Sleeping by Sebastian Litmanovich

SOUNDS AND COLOURS ARGENTINA

EDITOR
Russell Slater

ASSISTANT EDITORS
Danny Concha
Adam Fry
Nick MacWilliam
Matias Recharte

DESIGNER
Emma Canlin

COVER ART
Sandwich Gogogoch

TRANSLATIONS
Danny Concha, Adam Fry, Ellen Gordon, Alexandra Nataf and
Nicholas Nicou

CD PRODUCED BY
Concepto Cero and Sounds and Colours

THANKS
We'd like to say a special thanks to Pablo Bobadilla, Juan Data,
Adam Fry and George Kafka for their incredible support for the
project and their invaluable knowledge of Argentina. We'd like to
thank Lina Samoili for her help at the start of this project, Nicolas
Madoery and Ángel Clemente of Concepto Cero for being great
partners in producing the compilation, as well as Tim Castor,
Grant Dull, Leo Martinelli, Guillermo Piacenza, Diana Silva and
Nichola Smalley for their invaluable help along the way. Lastly,
we'd like to thank all of our contributors and funders, without
which this project would not have been possible.

SOUNDS AND COLOURS ARGENTINA is published by
Sounds and Colours

WEBSITE
www.soundsandcolours.com

EMAIL
info@soundsandcolours.com

GRACIAS

This book was made with the help of fundraisers who pre-ordered the book, along with a number of special Argentine perks, including postcards and posters. It's this kind of support and generosity that allows independent publishers like ourselves to keep taking risks and to know that there's an audience for niche projects such as this. We are hugely grateful that we get to keep making our Sounds and Colours publications and are eternally grateful for your support. We would therefore like to say a huge thanks (*gracias* in Spanish) to these great people:

A. Maya Pielak • Adam Fry • Adrian Potter • Alex King • Alexis Piquee • Amaya García-Velasco • Amy Story • Andrew Ashley Angus • Arsen Sogoyan • Caleb Connor • Callum Simpson Cameron Beauclerk • Carla Conte • Carolina Nunes • Christine Lofgren • Christine Slater • Claire Hutchinson • Damian Platt • Dan Williamson • David Dhannoo • David Horrocks • David Thomas • edwardiansnow • goatboy79 • Gordon Elcock • Jesse • Jim Zalles • Karin Lock • Karl Hildebrandt • Kathryn Cooper • Kosmas Chatzimichalis • Kristin Pouw • Lesley Wylie • Luis Ignacio • Matt Burnett • Matthew Slater • Matthias Koch • Michael Mannefeld nick • Nick Fitzgerald • Oliver Arditi • Oscar Arriagada • Pablo Navarrete • Paul Pasco • Pete Heskett • Richard Gustave • Richard Kemp • Robert Bresnan • Roberta Schwambach • Russell White Ryan Bestford • Sarah Jacobs • Slawomir Olszewski • Sophie Johnson • Sue Johnson • Thomas Glenn • Thomas Higinbotham Tim Lee • Wayne Gilbert • Will Stocker

CONTENTS

INTRODUCTION

by Russell Slater

We never planned on making a series of books about South American culture, but now that we're on to our fourth title (following Colombia, Brazil and Peru) it very much feels like we've fallen into that trap. It's a good job for us that each country has been able to offer up so many divergent paths for us to walk down and stumble around, making the challenge not how to fill each book but what we frustratingly have to leave out. Argentina has been no different.

As with previous titles, the idea has been to pick out some of our cultural icons from the country, but mainly to look between the cracks and find the hidden cliques where creativity thrives. Internationally Argentine culture is largely represented by its high-brow activities (tango, architecture, auteur cinema, literature) so we wanted to show that alongside its popular culture (cumbia, comic books, carnival), the culture of its indigenous and African-descended population and the big overlap between socio-political issues and culture that has had a huge impact on its street art, for example.

Argentina has a population of just over 40 million people, with the province of Greater Buenos Aires (which includes the city of Buenos Aires) accounting for almost 13 million of that figure (a third of the population). With that concentration it's perhaps unsurprising that Buenos Aires is the epicentre for many cultural movements coming out of Argentina. However, this is through convenience as much as anything else. For a country as vast as Argentina it's essential to have a gateway or meeting point for everything that's happening in the country and Buenos Aires serves the purpose well.

In recent years though curious Argentines have been travelling throughout their country more than ever, exploring its extraordinary landscapes, from the imposing grandeur of the Andes (switching between sparse tundra-esque white and vibrant green) to the timeless sparseness of the pampas and Tierra del Fuego. In addition, they've been exploring elements of their own folkloric, indigenous and Afro-Argentine culture that had been suppressed in the past. This curiosity has led to exciting new perspectives that can be found in cinema, literature, art and music, to name just a few mediums.

The book has been designed to offer you this journey through Argentina, beginning by focusing on Buenos Aires and its relationship with erudite and popular culture, with a heavy dose of *rock nacional*, but then starts to spread out its tentacles, touching on political issues that have inflicted people all over the country, to the cinema, literature and music of Patagonia in the south, to the cultural contributions of Afro-Argentineans and the country's indigenous population, to the folklore traditions of Cosquín and the underground movements happening in student-heavy cities like Rosario and La Plata, and on to the thirst for carnival in the north-east. Argentina is so much more than tango, Nobel laureates, Maradona, *mate* and a good steak.

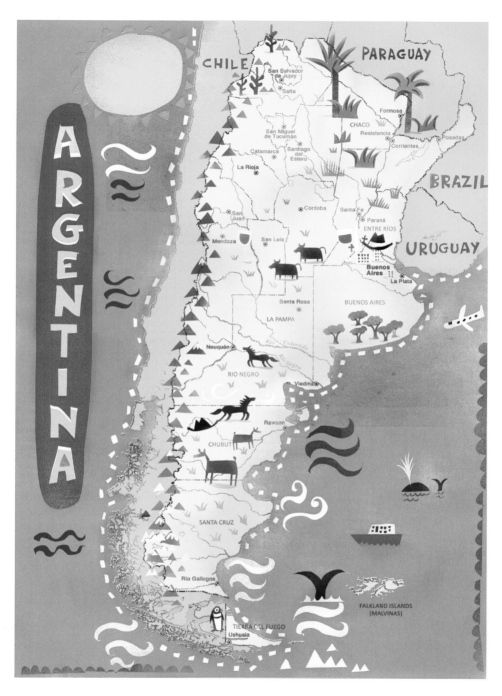

Argentina Map by Lee Hodges

ROCK, FOOTBALL AND STONES

ARGENTINA'S BARRIO PASSIONS

by Juan Data

In March 2016 Argentine rocker El Indio Solari, with his backing band Los Fundamentalistas Del Aire Acondicionado, broke all historic records when he summoned 150,000 paying fans to a concert in a remote, small town – a feat accomplished without corporate sponsors or major label support. No other rock star in Argentina's history can match the attendance of Solari's hugely massive events. However, while most other Argentine rock acts enjoy remarkable success across the Spanish-speaking world, El Indio Solari remains a local cult figure, exclusively known and appreciated by Argentine fans. And that's mainly because El Indio Solari belongs to a particular kind of impossible-to-export Argentine rock that makes very little sense outside of its Argentine context. In the mid 90s, when the genre reached massive status, music journalists labelled it *rock barrial*.

Rock barrial essentially means rock from the 'hood. It's a subgenre of *rock nacional* that appeals mainly to the disenfranchised youth of the impoverished, working-class outskirts of big cities like Buenos Aires. As a genre it's more easily recognizable by its fans, their peculiar aesthetics and social codes than the sonic attributes of the music, although, classic blues-based rock 'n' roll seem to be at the core of the genre's defining characteristics. Aesthetically *rock barrial* is utterly anti-glamorous. Even after reaching massive success, *rock barrial* artists aren't allowed to show off material gain or any spoils of fame, otherwise they'll lose their street cred and be considered traitors by their fans. Despite being intrinsically urban, intellectually and ideologically, the average *rock barrial* listener is closer to what in the US landscape would be a stereotypical country music fan than a hip-hop head. In fact, the only bragging that's allowed by *rock barrial* stars is to express how true to their *barrio* roots they remain. It's all about keeping it real and down to earth, unpretentious and unsophisticated, representing the everyday dude from down the street who wasn't born in a privileged socio-economic environment and arguably has a rather narrow world view.

THE ROOTS

In the mid 80s the so-called *rock nacional* became the most successful cultural export Argentina had to offer to the rest of the continent since tango. Pop/rock acts like Soda Stereo, Miguel Mateos, Los Enanitos Verdes and Los Fabulosos Cadillacs toured South and Central America, and Mexico spreading *rock en español* to crowds that welcomed them with open arms as genre pioneers who brought modern sounds to kids that previously had only local traditional and/or tropical pop to consume and identify with. It was a legit cultural revolution taking place across the continent.

In Argentina, however, that brand of rock quickly lost its revolutionary stance. The post-Falklands-war Argentine mainstream fully embraced *rock nacional* and it became the musical status quo of the average Argentine youth – it wasn't rebellious to be a rocker anymore, like it had been for the previous generations. It's worth mentioning that most of those rock acts that Argentina was exporting were from white/middle class backgrounds and fully embraced their social class' Eurocentric aesthetics. Meanwhile, an underground of local rockers that didn't quite fit that mould started cooking in the city's lower income neighbourhoods and built their identity in opposition to the establishment of *rock nacional*.

Electric blues guitar virtuoso Pappo is usually named as one of the pioneers of what would eventually become *rock barrial*. His old-school macho bravado, leather jacket and lyrics about cars and strip-clubs definitely resonated with a segment of the male youth that couldn't relate to the jet-set aspirations of the likes of Soda Stereo. However, it was Luca Prodan, the leader of the short-lived cult band Sumo, who would become, post-mortem, the poster-boy of the scene.

Born in Italy but educated in boarding schools in the UK, Prodan was in London in the late 70s when punk rock exploded and in the early 80s he relocated to Argentina hoping to kick off a heroin addiction. Heavily influenced by the British post-punk and reggae of the day, Prodan brought to Argentina's underground scene a completely different way of making rock music that diverted from the dominant 'poptimism' of the 80s *rock nacional* establishment as much as it did from the pretentiousness of the previous generation. Outside of a couple of major hits, Prodan never achieved superstardom in his lifetime (nor was that his intention) but soon after his death in 1987, and the consequential break-up of Sumo, he became a larger-than-life myth that permeated through all levels of Argentina's music underground and still remains vital today. His down-to-earth aesthetics and no-selling-out ethos became the top commandments of the *rock barrial* nation.

Two bands resulted from Sumo's dissolution, Divididos and Las Pelotas, and both would compete for top popularity in the *rock barrial* scene during the 90s and beyond. But the band that truly inherited the spirit of the departed Prodan, at least in the eyes of the fans, was Patricio Rey & Sus Redonditos De Ricota.

Led by the charismatic-while-reclusive Indio Solari, Patricio Rey & Sus Redonditos De Ricota (also known as Los Redondos, for short), embodied the rock resistance against the establishment by sticking to strict DIY politics: they never consented for their music to be used in commercials, they rejected all sponsors, never allowed managers or producers from outside the band's close-knit entourage to influence their decisions, they seldom gave interviews and only once in their whole career did they make a video clip. Somehow their unorthodox approach to rock, with cryptic lyrics full of surreal poetry, appealed directly to the kids in the city's impoverished outskirts who saw in Indio Solari a sort of reincarnation of Luca Prodan and started following him as the new *barrio* messiah. Paradoxically, despite Los Redondos' anti-commercial stance, by the mid 90s they would reach levels of popularity similar to the country's most profitable *rock nacional* acts, like Soda Stereo (widely considered their aesthetic nemesis.)

THE ROLINGA PHENOMENON

When it comes to pop music, Argentina has a thing for all things British – something quite paradoxical if we consider the post-Falklands war national resentment against the United Kingdom. And if one band epitomizes this national obsession it is, hands down, The Rolling Stones.

You could argue that The Rolling Stones are, and have always been, a global phenomenon and that they're amongst the all-time top five most popular rock acts world-wide. True, but you haven't seen anyone truly obsessed with The Rolling Stones until you meet Argentina's *rolingas*.

Somewhere around the late 80s a new scene started forming in Buenos Aires around one band, Los Ratones Paranoicos. Ratones were essentially a tribute band to The Rolling Stones who instead of doing covers wrote their own songs in Spanish, emulating the early style of Jagger and Richards. Their brand of rock had an un-questionable appeal with the *rock barrial* crowd and soon kids from all around the city's outskirts started dressing like them. A whole new fashion style that's uniquely Argentine emerged in the 90s associated with these kids who professed unidirectional devotion towards Their Satanic Majesties (who they perceive as the epitome of authentic, undiluted rock 'n' roll) and their Argentine clones. They called themselves *estón* or *rolingas* and they're easy to recognize because of their haircuts (mandatory bangs), flat canvas shoes combined with worn out denim, handkerchiefs tied around their necks and, of course, at least one Stones' logo printed on their T-shirt, jacket or skin.

Indio Solari, 2014 (photo by Efe de Mor)

In Argentina, when it comes to tribal social identities of youth, you can choose between being a punk rocker, a metal head, a raver, a *cumbiero*, a hip-hop junkie... or simply a *rolinga*. *Rolinga rock* is a whole self-contained scene within *rock barrial* and it's populated by an ever-growing list of bands who took the initial idea of Los Ratones Paranoicos to the next level by stripping it down even more, dumbing down the lyrics and simplifying

the song structures down to their very basics. *Rolinga rock*'s populist formula became synonymous with rock 'n' roll orthodoxy during the 90s, appealing to the lowest common denominator of a segment of the Argentine youth that suffered the most from the consequences of the decade's neo-liberal politics.

Some of the most iconic bands to emerge from the *rolinga* scene were Viejas Locas, Jóvenes Pordioseros and more recently La 25. Some others like, Los Piojos, gave their baby-steps in the *rolinga* format but eventually developed a more sophisticated style of their own that granted them access to the college crowds.

THE FOOTBALL CONNECTION

Other than the heirs to Sumo and the Rolling clones, there are other less abundant subspecies in the *rock barrial* ecosystem. Some lean heavily onto hard rock (La Renga), others merged the scene's aesthetics with punk rock (2 Minutos) and others do hybrid experiments with tropical rhythms and Argentine's own carnival music, *murga* (Bersuit Vergarabat). But they all have one thing in common: the adoption of football hooligan subculture.

There's a deep symbiotic relationship between *rock barrial* and Argentina's favourite pastime. *Rock barrial* fans bring football stadium habits to the concerts, including flags and fireworks and football hooligans bring *rock barrial* to the stadiums (it's not at all uncommon to see the Stones' tongue-and-lips logo hand-painted on football flags).

Argentine football fans are known for chanting long, elaborate songs that borrow their melodies of popular tunes and change the lyrics to root for their team or insult their rivals. In a country where there are no official radio charts, one of the most trusted indicators of a song's popularity can be its adoption by football fans. It's said that you haven't made it in Argentina's music business until one of your songs enters the stadium rotation.

Numerous *rock barrial* songs have been adapted into stadium chants since the early days of Sumo and Los Ratones Paranoicos but the influence is also noticeable in the opposite direction, *rock barrial* often borrowing inspiration from football and turning football anthems into rock songs (see Attaque 77's "Sola En La Cancha").

It's not at all uncommon to witness at *rock barrial* concerts, before the band comes on stage, the crowd chanting like football hooligans, but instead of rooting for their team they do so for the band in question... or they insult bands that they perceive as their opponents. Aware of this football-rock symbiosis, *barrial* rockers have often made songs about the sport with choruses that seem consciously predesigned to be adopted by the hooligans. And of course, a whole subgenre exists of *rock barrial* songs dedicated to the sport's messiah, Diego Maradona (Los Piojos' "Maradó" and Los Ratones Paranoicos "Para Siempre, Diego" are just a couple of examples).

THE DECLINE

In 2004 *rock barrial* made headlines even outside Argentina when a fire broke out at a Callejeros concert killing almost 200 attendees. Callejeros were the leaders of the new millennium's wave of *rock barrial* at the time and they played at an indoors venue in Buenos Aires where flares and fireworks were allegedly distributed by the band's entourage amongst the fans.

The tragedy marked a turning point for the genre. Not only did the genre become the focus of media criticism (some even prematurely declared the death of *rock barrial*), rock promoters and venues started refraining from booking *rock barrial* acts (the backlash indirectly affected rock acts from all genres). Some bands understandably distanced themselves from the scene, many others broke up in the years that followed the tragedy, and their lead singers reinvented themselves as solo artists detached from the genre's dominant mannerisms.

TV comedian Diego Capusotto became a viral sensation in 2006 with sketches that ridiculed the *rolinga* fan stereotype and the *rock barrial* stars (his popular character Pomelo was a mash-up between the lead singers of Los Ratones Paranoicos and Viejas Locas) and this also contributed to the downfall of the genre.

Meanwhile an overwhelming number of kids that were coming of age in those years in the working-class outskirts of Argentina's big cities didn't necessarily see *rock barrial* as the only outlet for their frustrations, instead they went for genres like *cumbia villera* and reggaeton. *Rock barrial*, however, survived and persists to the modern day as a last outpost of old school rock orthodoxy in a country that stubbornly clings to its rocker identity. And while the genre's undisputed patriarch, El Indio Solari, approaches his 70th birthday and threatens his fans with retirement, he still remains the biggest star in Argentina, summoning more people than all of his competitors combined.

Ruca Che arena in Neuquen during a Los Piojos concert, 2009 (photo by Diego Luciano)

AHEAD OF THE CURB

HOW ZZK RECORDS REDEFINED ELECTRONIC MUSIC IN LATIN AMERICA

by Amaya García-Velasco

It was a magical moment, even if no one really understood exactly what they were listening to. The year was 2008, when ZZK Records released its first compilation *ZZK Sounds Vol.1*, their introduction to the world outside of the Buenos Aires nightlife where they had begun. The hollow beats of the *bombo legüero*, the pulsating bassline and the triumphant "¡cumbia!" shout of Chancha Vía Circuito's opening track "Bosques Vía Temperley" could send shivers down anyone's spine, raise hairs on arms and quicken heartbeats. It was unlike any other music out there in the ether; the unmistakable signal that ZZK Records had arrived ready for a takeover of the DJ decks and mostly unaware of the switches they were about to flip, and the revolution they were about to become an integral part of.

"When Zizek started, we were in a strange place," explains Villa Diamante, founder and resident DJ of the Zizek Club parties. "Think about it this way: for the cumbia people, we were these rich kids. For electronic music people, we were the *negros cumbieros*. We were in a very strange place and nobody really understood our place within the music scene." Musicologists, most notably Fabian Holt, call this state the poetics of the in-between, a categorical limbo that allows those situated within it the power of decentred thinking, the ability to take what they want from different genres and bend it to their will. It's about transformation and movement, a fact that was not lost on the collective's founders: Grant C. Dull, Villa Diamante, and DJ Nim. "Part of our success is that we're able to have one foot in all these different worlds," Dull says. "We're in the electronic world, in the Latin world, in world music, a bit in the urban world. We're able to touch different music lovers, different styles and different tastes."

Using cumbia as a platform to jump off of, the ZZK collective managed to rally those artists and producers willing to launch themselves head on into uncharted territory in Argentina --to deconstruct their roots and propel them into the 21st century, mixing them with the popular genres they know and love in the process. What started as an Argentine experiment, has become, ten years later, an unapologetically Latin American thing, achieving what predecessors like Mexico's Nortec Collective stopped just short of doing years before it disbanded: a homegrown electronic music with the potential to truly go 'worldwide', not as a weird novelty, but as a force to be reckoned with. The influence of the ZZK way of thinking now spans far and wide. From Buenos Aires to Montreal, New York, Mexico City, Bogotá, Quito, Lima and the Caribbean, there are countless electronica scenes and artists that would not exist without that initial seed: the desire to destabilize the dance floor.

IN THE BEGINNING, THERE WAS ZIZEK

"I found a notebook from 2006 with something written like three months before Zizek [Club] started, that said: "My concern is the dance floor," recounts Villa Diamante. "It was a treatise detailing the things that concerned me about the dance floor back then, which was to decentralize and de-structure. Here in Argentina, if you go to a rock bar, you only hear rock. When you go to a *bailanta*, you only hear cumbia. It's all genre-based, so my idea was 'why not break with the genres'. If we like to dance, then let's dance to music in general, we don't have to be so close-minded. So, when Zizek started, the initial approach that Grant, DJ Nim and I worked out was: if hip hop, cumbia, electronica and reggaeton have similar dance moves, why not start a club night that can hold all these together?"

In mid-2000s Argentina, Villa Diamante's proposal may well have been a fever dream: a dance music utopia where everybody reconvened after a hard day to dance, no matter what the style or genre. The reality was starkly different as Buenos Aires, a city with a vibrant club scene, had suddenly shut down due to a tragic fire at the República Cromañón nightclub where 194 people died and countless others were injured. This was close to New Year's Eve in 2004, and this left everyone (the people and the government) scrambling to find a culprit and deeply hurt by the loss of young lives, specifically rock fans. For a city that had become a synonym for rock music, the loss was especially devastating. The disaster at the Cromañón triggered a storm that led to the eventual arrests and trials of the club's manager, promoters, band managers, police officers and city officials, and a flurry of government reforms. The most notable of these was the 'no dancing' law, one that Villa Diamante recalls was violently enforced. "Everything was criminalized: dancing, rock, live music," he says.

"Before Cromañón, I used to play at a lot of illegal parties in people's houses, in clothing stores, art galleries that doubled as venues. But, after that, everything suddenly closed," he continues. "There were no possibilities of playing anywhere because you were quickly shut down." Months of prohibition and fear led to a complex cultural situation in Buenos Aires that became the fuel for Dull, DJ Nim and Villa Diamante to set up Zizek Club. Dull, an American immigrant, had become a fixture in the Buenos Aires nightlife due to his website 'What's Up Buenos Aires', a cultural journal designed to highlight the emerging arts and culture scene in the city. After the website caught traction, Dull began curating parties and, incidentally, became an events producer and promoter.

"About a year and a half later, I started working with DJ Nim and we started throwing some parties together that went really well," Dull recounts. "Then, for one party we got Villa Diamante on board and that was kind of the first time the three Zizek guys met and threw a party together." After those initial successes, DJ Nim explains he proposed to Dull to work on a cycle of parties together. They started on a Wednesday slot in a club in the San Telmo district, with a focus on underground sounds: reggaeton, dancehall, hip hop. "I was a DJ as well, but I didn't really know how to add myself as a resident,"

The Zizek crew (Villa Diamante is in yellow)

DJ Nim says. While Nim's musical inclinations (obscure and experimental electronica) were more suited for a wind-down set, Villa Diamante's mash-ups were a perfect mix to unhinge the dance floor. "He came on board and he brought this other side which is bastard pop, cumbia, folklore, and all the stuff he was doing at the time," Dull remarks. "Within ten days, we had formed this concept where we wanted to put on blast all the different producers that were experimenting with local sounds and making their own music, and create this weekly party around that."

Thus Zizek Club was born, named after the Slovenian philosopher who, according to Dull, represented what they were trying to achieve: "blend the old with the new, the contemporary with the folkloric and the crazy with the normal."

THE HOUSE THAT DIGITAL CUMBIA BUILT

Without digital cumbia, Zizek Club would've been just another pop music shindig and ZZK Records would not exist as we now know it today. Perhaps both might've looked like completely different ventures, and no one knows if they would've had the niche success and the cultural gravitas they both forged. One thing is clear: you can't talk about anything related to the collective without talking about the rise of digital cumbia as a legitimate electronic music genre, born and raised in urban South America and with enough solid power to become its own system within the global bass universe, spawning subgenre after subgenre everywhere from Buenos Aires to South Africa. Even though some form of digital cumbia has existed since the mid-90s, when it comes to defining its now characteristic sound, Zizek Club (and later ZZK Records) quickly became ground zero; the think tank where the music would come to be refined. It was also where its highly intellectual discourse was inadvertently hatched via the group's curatorial practices which assured, not only the quality of the music, but the quality of the overall proposal. Nothing was rushed. It became a lesson in organic growth: if the music and the idea behind the music was good, the rest would follow.

"We wanted to look for the new scene," Villa Diamante recalls. "The first month was kind of a free for all, we had a little bit of everything. But what happened was that all the people doing dancehall, hip hop and stuff like that were almost a copy of what was going on in other places. It wasn't very authentic. In our search for new stuff Grant, Nim and I realised that the people producing a truly new sound were doing cumbia. That's how we ended up featuring El Remolón, Chancha Vía Circuito, King Coya, Fauna and Frikstailers." It is no coincidence that these artists would become part of the initial roster of ZZK Records and would feature heavily in the compilation *ZZK Sound Vol. 1*, a genre defining moment that would become the label's calling card. According to the trio, they were all friendly faces, artists and collaborators that they already admired, who they were exchanging mp3s with, who were friends with them on MySpace and Photolog. Among them were also Marcelo Fabian, Oro 11 and Fantasma, who rounded out the tracklist for ZZK Records' debut in 2008.

"*ZZK Sound Vol.1 Cumbia Digital* is where we were basically showing the world, in a different format, what was happening at the club nights weekly," Dull adds. "We kind of grabbed all the best tracks from all the different producers we were working with, created this compilation and launched the record label." At the time, this was also the debut of the term digital cumbia, which Dull says came to life in a similar fashion to the name ZZK: incidentally. Electro-cumbia was already a well established genre and 'digital cumbia' seemed to encapsulate the ethos of the music, which is mostly made with computers and digital instruments. From his end, DJ Nim approached it through his expertise: dancehall. "As a student of the music of Jamaica, I recognized the point of inflection in dancehall reggae through the Sleng Teng riddim (an instrumental beat made exclusively with a digital keyboard). That's when it officially started calling itself digital dancehall. I saw the similarities and realized *cumbia digital* described this music perfectly," he explained.

The ZZK crew united under the digital cumbia banner a myriad of projects that, while having cumbia as a starting point, veered wildly in their approaches to it. ZZK Records' first signee, Fauna (later renamed Faauna) created a raucous mixture of dancehall reggae, drum 'n' bass and *cumbia villera* that resulted in the label's first full length by a single artist, *La Manita de Fauna*. It was an undeniably raunchy, energetic, bass-heavy music, refined two years later for their second album *Manshines*. As a result of touring through South America and Europe, Fauna began transmuting their sound to add *kuduro* and dubstep, before the untimely death of one of its founding members, Catar_sys. The Córdoba duo Frikstailers went a similar route, intersecting cumbia with synth pop, hip hop, tribal and techno under a futuristic theme, constantly evolving to include regional Andean sounds such as *murga* while maintaining a dance floor ready vibe. Chiptune group Super Guachin, Villa Diamante, Lagartijeando, King Coya and El Remolón round out the roster with their own cumbia- and even reggaeton-inflected party-ready jams. Nonetheless, King Coya and El Remolón, slowly but surely, would bleed their music into the labels most groundbreaking camp: experimental digital cumbia.

Throughout *Pibe Cosmo*, El Remolón established his brand of digital cumbia as of the minimal variety, stripping down his influences (reggaeton, minimal techno, dub) to its bare essentials. For *Cumbias de Villa Donde*, King Coya stressed on the downtempo, not so much drowning the cumbia and folkloric rhythms in synths and bass, but highlighting them and bringing out their electronic capacity in an understated way. El Remolón moved on to compose one of the first digital cumbia original soundtracks for the film *Boxeo Constitución*, and Gaby Kerpel has gone on to not only tour and refine King Coya's live act, but to compose music for the show *Fuerza Bruta* and to arrange actual cumbias for another ZZK act, La Yegros.

Tremor was one of the first acts on the label to come from the glitch and IDM worlds, creating on their first effort *Viajante* a heady, minimalistic digital cumbia better suited for headphones, that incorporated samples of live instrumentation. It was a cinematic approach, one that Chancha Vía Circuito would further develop. He arrived a short time after with *Rodante*, but it wasn't until 2011's *Río Arriba* that he gained notoriety for his take on the genre. That whole album is an impressive feat, a study in the respectful transformation and deconstruction of folklore, and one that set a precedent for future producers who would grow up to be influenced by the music of Chancha, like Ecuadorian Nicolá Cruz. But, what mostly stuck in people's heads was his rework of "Quimey Neuquén", José Larralde's Andean classic, which he turned into a sparse, bass-heavy introspection into the region's folklore. The track ran around the world, most notably being placed in a key scene for AMC's drug drama, *Breaking Bad*. The success of Chancha Vía Circuito proved to be a pivotal point for ZZK Records, inadvertently gaining its founders a privileged view of where the digital cumbia sound was heading.

I find it interesting that, sonically, the road newer artists – whether they belong to the ZZK roster or are producing a similar sound – are leading themselves towards is going full circle, leading back to deeper, more nuanced explorations of folkloric music, and not just from Argentina. Animal Chuki, for example, operates in Lima and constantly references Peruvian folklore and Amazonian psychedelia. Nicolá Cruz explores the Ecuadorian Andes, and the whole gang united to remix a portion of Luzmila Carpio's repertoire of Bolivian folk songs sung in Quechua, with her blessing. In a world that continues to rapidly draw and violently enforce frontiers (social, economic, political and cultural) ZZK Records' united front is inspiring, rallying the most forward-thinking minds to push the different South American cultures forward, with the value, care and personal investment that they so deserve.

This responsibility is not taken lightly, and that's another point towards ZZK's success. They've been challenging everyone, most notably the music press, to stop being lazy, to listen carefully and to go back to the drawing board if they need to in order to understand where these artists are coming from. Perhaps most importantly, to relearn things (whether it be about cumbia, the music of Ecuador or even the staples of electronic music) and let old umbrella categories take a backseat. In a recent Facebook rant regarding the 'global bass' tag, the founder of the Portuguese Enchufada label Branko, said it best: "We're making electronic music rooted in different geographical coordinates that intends to spread other perspectives of the world through a very DIY environment, showing that everyone with a great idea and some cracked software no matter when/where/how can make relevant music. For me, that's what's beautiful about this movement."

ON REMAINING AHEAD OF THE CURB

Relevance is a continuous challenge in any venture, but it is specifically daunting when it comes to electronic music, where styles, genres and sounds disappear as quickly as they come to life. You're damned if your music is weak, flash in the pan fare, but you're not necessarily guaranteed success if you're too cutting edge. The ZZK crew was a few years ahead of its time. From its 'blank slate' curating practices, to organising their vision and championing artistic musical freedom, their method to ride the wave has guaranteed them breathing room for sonic growth and brand growth, if not always economic gain. "Being ahead of the curb is a good place to be," Dull remarks. "It's not an easy place to be, neither financially nor culturally, but it's a good place to be because

19

you are able, slowly but surely, to start knocking down little walls and spreading to bigger audiences."

Ten years after that first party in San Telmo, the ZZK crew can officially lay claim to a generation of producers all across Latin America and Europe who have grown up with, and even been taught by, the first wave of the ZZK school: El Remolón, Chancha Vía Circuito, Frikstailers and the like. The second wave, spearheaded by El Búho, Barrio Lindo, Animal Chuki and Nicolá Cruz and labeled ZZK 2.0, is stronger than ever and even more diverse, focusing their energies on creating original beats that highlight other Latin American musical enclaves. As Dull explains, ZZK's all-round vision has always encouraged, if not required, a natural deviation from cumbia into a wider folkloric territory. If it's electronic and Latin American, ZZK welcomes it with open arms. "Since the whole digital cumbia thing, we've just kind of been inspired by things that people send us," adds Dull. "We're just evolving with the scene. We're not pushing it in any specific direction. When somebody like Nicolá Cruz comes around and creates this new genre [Andes step], this new exploration from this different country, that's gonna have a trickle effect. Of course, him being in the limelight a little bit, it's gonna push the scene into different places. We just watch it evolve, naturally."

This evolution has led Dull to create two other ZZK divisions to document and support the artists they work with, but also to remain afloat. Recently, ZZK Records was about to go bankrupt and the crew resorted to the crowdfunding platform Indiegogo to save the label. The campaign was a success, allowing for the creation of ZZK Films. The first of its products is an ambitious documentary series called *The Nu Lat Am Sound*, focused on profiling music scenes across Latin America, and the second, a full length feature called *A Musical Journey*, documenting La Yegros' month-long tour across Europe. But Dull has his eye set on one of ZZK's biggest projects yet, AYA Records, a venture geared towards highlighting the work of live bands. "AYA Records is going to be contemporary Latin American music across the board," he says. "We're not confining ourselves to electronic interpretations of Latin American music, we want to just kind of open up the doors."

Their run is just beginning but, so far, the open door policy is the ultimate legacy the ZZK crew has left for the Argentine music scene and the Latin American electronic music scene. The PLUR mantra [Peace, Love, Unity, Respect] in its real world application; imperfect yet attainable. "These past ten years have had a very important influence on the *porteño* scene," concludes DJ Nim. "Now we have a second and even a third wave of artists inspired by these sounds, but we're subtly influencing other artists in more established genres. They're not as fearful to start making cumbia, or electronic artists that aren't as fearful to incorporate it [in their music]. Certain taboos and rules that marked natural territories have been irreversibly broken."

Inroducing Ezequiel Garcia

In this book you will find two comic strips by Argentine comic book author Ezequiel Garcia. After receiving classes by Alberto Breccia (an influential illustrator from the Golden Age of Argentine comics), Garcia began making comics for international and national publications, as well as co-editing collections of comic strips, from the mid-90s onwards.

In 2007 he published the graphic novel *Llega A Los 30* (Reaching Thirty), followed by *Creciendo En Público* in 2013, the latter of which was published in English with the title *Growing Up In Public* in 2016. Both novels offer a highly-personal take on life in Buenos Aires, documenting Ezequiel's close relationships with music, art and culture, and the many relationships and friendships that come and go while living in a big city.

In this book you can find an excerpt of *Growing Up In Public* (p. 22-29) and a brand new English translation (by Ellen Gordon) of the short story *Creciendo En Público – Museum of Cinema* (p. 124-127) produced especially for this publication.

As well as creating graphic novels and comic stripes, these days Ezequiel is a teacher, fanzine and magazine editor, curator and member of the Un Faulduo collective.

THE ADVENTURES OF LAURA & EZEQUIEL in THE CONTEMPORARY ART WORLD

HI! SORRY I'M LATE!

IT'S OK, I JUST GOT HERE.

SHALL WE?

OF COURSE!

SO HOW'S IT GOING?

FINE. AND YOU?

ALL RIGHT... I JUST MET UP WITH A FRIE WHO TOLD ME ABOU THE OPERA THEATRE OUTRAGE...

IN 1931, THE PALAIS DE GLACE BECAME THE HEADQUARTERS FOR THE NATIONAL DEPARTMENT OF FINE ARTS. NOW IT'S USED AS A GALLERY. MOUNTING AN EXHIBIT THERE ISN'T EASY SINCE IT WASN'T DESIGNED FOR THAT PURPOSE. THE PLACE IS GENERALLY REGARDED AS BUENOS AIRES' WORST EXHIBITION SPACE. BUT IT'S RUN BY THE GOVERNMENT, SO IT BELONGS TO ALL OF US...

BLA BLA BLA BLA BLA

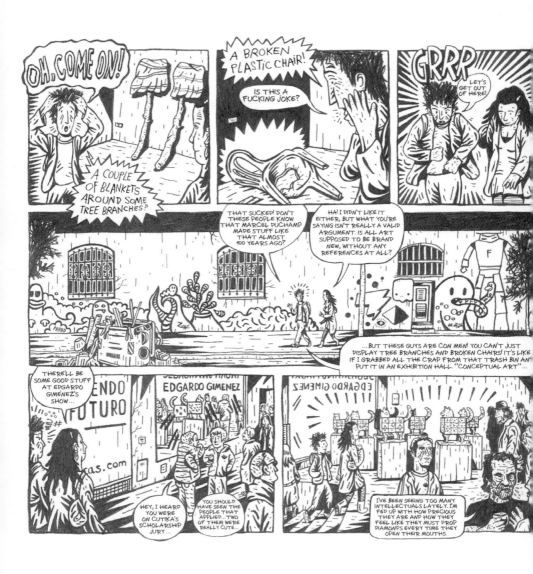

24

25

HA HA HA!

EDGARDO, EXCUSE ME...

WELL KIDS, I'VE GOT TO GO...

I'LL CALL YOU TOMORROW, PIGEON, AND WE'LL TALK ABOUT EVERYTHING FROM A TO Z...

OK!

HE'S AMAZING, ISN'T HE?

YES, ABSOLUTELY TERRIFIC.

DO YOU WANT TO GET SOMETHING TO EAT?

HAVE YOU NOTICED THE CRAP THEY'RE BUILDING RIGHT HERE?

YEAH, IT'S A PITY. THIS WAS A NICE BLOCK.

DESTRUYENDO TU FUTURO

www.edificiosgarcas.com

EG

PIRPIP

HERE'S A TEXT FROM RAFA. THERE'S A PARTY IN ABASTO. SHOULD WE GO?

I LIKED LAURA MORE AND MORE EVERY MINUTE. SHE WASN'T REALLY MY TYPE — BUT SHE DAZZLED ME.

WE CAN DECIDE LATER, RIGHT?

LAURA HAD SOMETHING...SPECIAL. SHE WAS MORE REAL TO ME SOMEHOW. AND THAT WAS GOOD. BETTER THAN CHASING AFTER THOSE UNREACHABLE GLITTERING "STARS" THAT I ALWAYS SEEMED TO FALL IN LOVE WITH.

...AND IN TWO WEEKS I'M LEAVING FOR COLOMBIA.

REALLY? WHAT FOR?

I'M GOING WITH MY FRIEND AS PART OF AN ARTIST EXCHANGE WITH THE UNIVERSITY OF ANTIOQUIA IN MEDELLÍN. WE'LL EXHIBIT OUR WORK AND GIVE A TALK...

THAT'S GREAT!

*ANTONIO BERNI (1905—1981), ONE OF ARGENTINA'S MOST FAMOUS ARTISTS.

28

FORMER MEMBERS OF THE ARMY AND THE SECRET SERVICES WERE ON TRIAL FOR TORTURE AND MURDER COMMITTED AT THE
AUTOMOTORES ORLETTI, A SECRET TORTURE CENTER RUN BY THE GOVERNMENT DURING ARGENTINA'S LAST DICTATORSHIP.
ESMA (THE ESCUELA SUPERIOR DE MECÁNICA DE LA ARMADA), RUN BY
ARGENTINA'S NAVY, WAS ANOTHER SECRET TORTURE CENTER.

BRUTALIST BUILDINGS

THE PIONEERING ARCHITECTURE OF CLORINDO TESTA

by George Kafka

photos by Alan Chac

On 22nd March 2016, 240 employees of the Biblioteca Nacional (National Library) of Argentina were laid off. For those losing their jobs – around a quarter of the library's workforce – this was a catastrophic day met with fainting and nervous breakdowns, while for the wider Argentinean population it was yet another in a series of brutal public sector cuts that characterized the opening months of Mauricio Macri's tenure as President.

The effects of Macri's austerity economics has been felt, and opposed, by Argentineans across the spectrum of the public sector – particularly those working in healthcare and government offices. Yet there is a specific potency to the library cuts, made manifest by the very structure that houses the now-empty offices alongside the collective knowledge of the nation: the library building itself.

Designed by Clorindo Testa in 1961, the brutalist Biblioteca Nacional at Aguero 2502, Buenos Aires is an astonishing sight. Passing by on foot, one cannot help but stop and stare in awe at the hulking eruption of concrete that sits amidst the neo-baroque facades of the Recoleta neighbourhood. Yet get closer to the beast, and you discover a certain tenderness beyond its rough appearance; curved walkways, subtle colouring of details and a generous public garden make the library more of a gentle giant than a looming monstrosity. More than anything, the structure is a monument to public education and civic pride.

That this building was cast in an explicitly brutalist manner should come as no surprise. Like his Banco de Londres and the subterranean tombs at the Chacarita Cemetery, the use of rough, untreated *béton brut* (from which the term brutalism comes) elaborated with dramatic cantilevers and perforated structural elements is typical of Testa's particular brand of brutalism. The style is currently going through something of a digital renaissance, often manifesting itself in the online glorification of abandoned Soviet structures, which tends to overlook the ethics behind the 'brutal' aesthetic.

Brutalism came to prominence in post-war Europe, when socialist values were influencing everything from healthcare to housing. With its exposed functional

unpretentious materials and a quick, often cheap construction process, brutalism was the ideal way to express new and more egalitarian societal values in built form. Apartment blocks, hospitals, universities and cultural centres cast in rough concrete and expressive forms appeared across Europe, most notably with Le Corbusier's Unite D'Habitation in Marseille (1953), Ernö Goldfinger's Trellick Tower and Denys Lasdun's National Theatre, both in London (1972 & 1976). Heavily inspired by the work of Le Corbusier, Testa's successful proposal for the National Library building in Buenos Aires (designed in partnership with architects Francisco Bullrich and Alicia Cazzaniga) came in 1961, at the height of the style's popularity.

However, a lengthy and controversial construction process – interrupted by political instability, the dictatorship and the lack of priority afforded cultural infrastructure

Banco de Londres y América del Sur

— meant that the library's foundation stone was not laid until 1971. Even then, it wasn't officially opened until 1992, by which point architectural trends and political priorities had shifted wholesale. That it was infamous neo-liberal President Carlos Menem who oversaw the opening ceremony of the library indicates the extent of the cultural and political transformations that had taken place in the time between design and completion; Menem's legacy in the built environment of Buenos Aires is limited to the austere glass and steel of Puerto Madero, an architecture of isolation, exclusivity and inequality.

Perhaps no structure exemplifies the effect of political shifts on architecture more than the Banco de Londres y América del Sur. Designed in 1959 and completed by 1966 the building fitted more neatly into the brutalist aesthetic of the era than the Biblioteca

Nacional. That said, fitting it into the gridlock of downtown Buenos Aires was much more of a challenge, and one that Testa met with ingenuity. The bank is hugely sensitive to its surroundings, not only mirroring the height and shape of the pre-existing block in reference to its neoclassical neighbours, but also in facilitating local street life: the building's main entrance is set back within a cut-off corner, creating a small public square, and the surrounding facade walls overhang the pavements, leaving extra room for passing pedestrians. Add to this its large windows and perforated elements on the multilayered facade and the bank appears part streetscape and part public sculpture.

When considered in contrast to the impenetrable and sterile glass and steel of Puerto Madero's neo-liberal architecture, the true value of the Banco de Londres is made clear. That a bank should be designed along brutalist lines at all is highly unusual (brutalism is most typically associated with public institutions: universities, libraries, theatres), let alone one which displays such openness and sensitivity to its surroundings. This is made all the more pertinent by considering the negative reputation that brutalism had acquired throughout decades of unpopularity, being labelled as isolating, disorienting and even dystopian. Indeed, as architectural critic Jack Self argues, "The brutalist citizen [...] has to be understood as an abstract egalitarian ideal, not (as is more commonly portrayed) an individual lost in a microscopic concrete cave of some gargantuan homogenous facade." With the open facades and public spirit of the Biblioteca Nacional and the Banco de Londres we see the opposite to be true.

Testa's egalitarian brutalism is never clearer than at the Chacarita Cemetery, where his subterranean catacombs do away with facades completely. Instead, an intertwined complex of stairways, gardens and niche-filled walls snakes underground to provide shelter to the city's deceased. The Chacarita cemetery is relatively

Banco de Londres y América del Sur

unknown to tourists, who tend to flock to the flagship tombs of Recoleta Cemetery. There, the extravagant tombs of famous figures and families jostle for attention with polished black marble and decaying neoclassicism. The Chacarita cemetery on the other hand is more often associated with working class *porteños* and folk heroes such as Carlos Gardel and Gustavo Cerati, and this is reflected in Testa's design. Beneath flat-roofed entrance pavilions, staircases descend to corridors of *columbaria*, with niches differentiated by the small photographs and flowers left by grieving families. At the end of the corridors, large voids allow sunlight to pour from ground level down to pseudo-plazas. Rough, untreated concrete is, once again, the predominant material.

To descend the divergent staircases at the cemetery is to step into a quiet space of reflection, where beams of sunlight dance through perforated walls and *porteños* lie shoulder to shoulder. Dignity for both the deceased and visiting families, as opposed to ostentatious displays of status, is the predominant theme of Testa's Chacarita.

Yet, perhaps paradoxically, there is also a utopian impulse behind the structure. With its open squares and wide corridors it resembles something between an inverted Barbican Centre and a necropolitan cityscape. Testa was working in the city department

Chacarita Cemetery

for urbanism at the time of the structure's completion in 1956 and one cannot help but feel that working on this project allowed him to experiment with his vision for an ideal city: yet one populated by corpses instead of citizens. At Chacarita, Testa lays out an architecture of striking dignity and hope amidst the melancholia of a cemetery.

Contradictory, yes, but it is this sense of contrast, juxtaposition and collage that is so fascinating about Argentina. In Testa's architecture we see something inherently Argentinean – a style and aesthetic adapted from Europe and carried forward through bold statements: a cemetery of hope for the living; a brutalist bank open to its pedestrian passers; and a library which protrudes into the *porteño* sky as a statement of solidarity with its citizens.

The built environment is always subject to political whims and cultural shifts. Not even the heavyset concrete tree that is the Biblioteca Nacional will last forever. Yet while it continues to overlook the Río de la Plata, it remains as a symbol of hope for the collective cultural value of a people that will outlast the legacy of any Menem or Macri. The legacy of Clorindo Testa, the Argentinean architect par excellence, is that of the Argentinean people.

Chacarita Cemetery

SAMPA VS BUENOS

TWO LATIN AMERICAN CITIES GO HEAD TO HEAD

by Vivian Mota

"In 2012 I had the idea to create the **Sampa Versus Buenos** project. I was familiar with Paris vs. New York, a project created by the graphic designer Vahran Muratyan and I was a fan of his. That's why, during a trip to Buenos Aires, I thought about doing something similar for São Paulo and Buenos Aires, mainly because it would be fun. During the project, I noticed that there were many things that these two cities have in common.

The selection of images was done very intuitively. At first, I drew icons that were familiar to me and later they came through research and suggestions."

These illustrations compare iconic images from Buenos Aires (top image) with similar emblems from São Paulo (bottom image).

tango

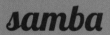

samba

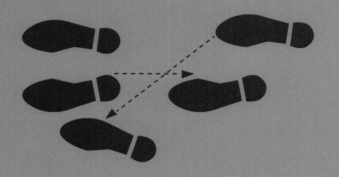

alpargatas

havaianas

locro

feijoada

bondi

busão

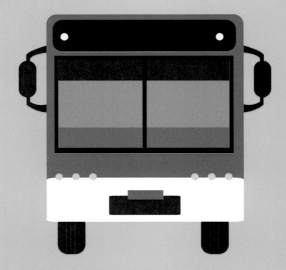

KODAMA VS KATCHADJIAN

A BORGESIAN WRANGLE AT EVERY LEVEL

by Claire Green

In Jorge Luis Borges' celebrated short story "The Aleph" (El Aleph, 1949), the narrator notes of his friend Carlos Argentino Daneri's work that "only the fear of creating an army of implacable and powerful enemies dissuaded him (he told me) from fearlessly publishing this poem." It appears that the university professor Pablo Katchadjian did not share this fear when he published his *El Aleph Engordado*; a re-worked, expanded, 'fattened-up' version of the original story, published some sixty years later... and create enemies he did, particularly in the implacable, powerful form of Borges' widow and owner of his estate, Maria Kodama. Thus begins the ongoing legal battle over questions of plagiarism, intertextuality and authorship more reminiscent of Borges' writing than its intellectual property status. Yet, despite all its literary flourishes this case has had significant real-life implications for Katchadjian, who could face up to six years imprisonment if convicted of intellectual property fraud. The case sends out a message to others who may wish to 'play' with this most playful of Argentine writers.

El Aleph Engordado was published in 2009 in the independent journal IAP (Imprenta Argentina de Poesía), with a run of just 200 copies. As its title suggests, it is a reworking of Borges' story which consisted in adding to, rather than editing, the original narrative: Katchadjian added around 5,600 words to the existing 4,000. This principle was so integral to Katchadjian's project that he states it as the only criterion in his postscript, writing that "the work of fattening-up had only one rule: not to remove nor alter anything of the original text, not words, not commas, not full-stops, not the order. This means that Borges' text is intact but totally crisscrossed with mine, meaning that, if anyone wanted to, they could return to Borges' text from this one." This faithfulness to the original text means that Katchadjian's work is largely about expanding upon the subtler features which are hinted at by Borges. For example, in a passage describing photographs of the narrator's deceased friend Beatriz Viterbo, Borges notes one showing "Beatriz, soon after her divorce, at a luncheon at the Turf Club," to which Katchadjian adds "...surrounded by men." Similarly, Katchadjian elaborates on Borges' description of Beatriz as "tall, frail, slightly stooped" with the supplementary image that this slight stoop was 'like an Italian tower.' The latter's characterization of Carlos Argentino Daneri is also far more detailed and in-depth, although like that of Beatriz it plays upon rather than diverts Borges' original hints.

However, other additions signify a more significant re-working and interpretation of the original text. Katchadjian's Daneri states that on seeing the Aleph in his basement he finally came to understand the Fibonacci sequence. This notion is not referenced in the story itself but instead draws on a wider analysis of the author, particularly in relation to his concept of the infinite library. By alluding to Borges' theme, Katchadjian may not only be knowingly referencing his own project but also invoking a sense of permission from Borges himself. Borges' concept of the infinite library, explored at great length in the short story "The Library of Babel" (La Biblioteca de Babel, 1941) and essay "The Total Library" (La Biblioteca Total, 1939), reflects a long-standing interest in subverting concepts of infinity, chronology, possible worlds and symbolic sequences. This interest is often manifested in Borges' work through mathematics, such as the fractal geometry of "The Garden of Forking Paths" (El Jardín de Senderos que se Bifurcan, 1941), the interconnected hexagonal galleries of the aforementioned "Library of Babel", or the almost algebraic linguistic ordering system of "The Analytical Language of John Wilkins" (El Idioma Analitico de John Wilkins, 1952). Thus Katchadjian's reference to Fibonacci, raises his project somewhat above the text itself and into the world of Borges Studies; whether the addition is intended to invoke posthumous permission from Borges, to assure the reader that Katchadjian has done his homework, or merely to add another level of intrigue to the project, it certainly seems to transform *El Aleph Engordado* from a work of literature into a piece of literary theory.

This sense of 'permission' from Borges is bolstered by the fact that his interest in infinity was often expressed through literary as well as mathematical themes. This is clear in "The Aleph" itself, which intertwines issues of writing and literary talent with questions of infinity, immanence and universes within universes. As the first letter of the Hebrew alphabet and the number one in the same language, the Aleph is a symbol of infinity and of everything; it is surely no coincidence that Katchadjian used Borges' window onto the universe as a window onto Borges. Along with this example, "The Total Library" and "The Library of Babel", Borges linked books, writing and literature with infinity in stories such as "Pierre Menard, Author of the Quixote" (1939) and the essay "Kafka and his Precursors" (1951). Both texts raise pertinent issues surrounding the *El Aleph Engordado* controversy. In the latter, Borges subverts conventional understanding of chronology and influence to argue that "every writer creates his own precursors. His work modifies our conception of the past, as it will modify the future". This could be seen to endorse a writer's retrospective engagement with their literary inheritance, modifying conceptions of their work in the way Katchadjian has "The Aleph". Furthermore, in his essay Borges admits engaging with Kafka in this manner despite previously considering him to be "as singular as the phoenix of rhetorical praise": a position not dissimilar from that which Borges is now seen to occupy, as the great elder statesman of the Argentine literary canon. This aura of untouchability surrounding Borges may have contributed to Katchadjian's work seeming so bold to Kodama, and it is precisely that sense of sacrosanct singularity which Borges himself plays with in "Kafka and his Precursors".

The theme of reworking or readdressing classic literature is also integral to Borges' short story "Pierre Menard, Author of the Quixote". Borges describes the fictional writer Menard and his entirely faithful, "word for word and line for line" rewriting of parts of Cervantes' *Don Quixote*. Despite his exact reproduction of Cervantes' text, the narrator finds that Menard has composed an innovative and more interesting Quixote through the difference in his native language and period compared to those of Cervantes. Through this exercise, the narrator suggests, he "has (perhaps unwittingly) enriched the slow and rudimentary art of reading by means of a new technique – the technique of deliberate anachronism and fallacious attribution". Whilst Katchadjian's stated intention and postscript spare him from the accusation of 'fallacious attribution', part of the enjoyment of *El Aleph Engordado* is found in the confusion over whether a particular phrase comes from Borges or Katchadjian which may be felt by any reader who does not know the original by rote. This effect is highlighted by Katchadjian in his postscript, where he states that "with respect to my writing, while I did not intend to hide behind Borges' style, nor did I write with the intention of making myself too visible: the best moments, it seems to me, are those in which it can't be said with certainty what is by who". As such, while Katchadjian makes it explicit that he is not claiming Borges' words or style as his own, it is clear that part of the innovation and interest to the reader is the obfuscation and melding of the two narrative voices. Against the backdrop of Borges' own exploration of the themes of nonlinear authorship, recurrence and the infinite interaction of literature described above, the enjoyment for the reader becomes twofold; in the uncertainty of reading "The Aleph" 'fattened-up' in this manner and in considering how this relates to the wider canon of Borges' own work.

However, the question currently being played out in Argentina's Cámara Nacional de Casación Penal, the country's highest court of criminal appeal, is not whether Katchadjian's experiment has literary merit but whether it is fraudulent. Katchadjian is no longer standing trial, since an appeal in August 2015 which revoked the 80,000 peso fine he had been handed, and annulled the trial on the basis of lack of merit. Nevertheless, the author has still not been vindicated; the dismissal of the case requested by Katchadjian's lawyers was not granted, and the court has ordered a specialist report to investigate and compare his work with Borges' original. Kodama claims this report will show Katchadjian did in fact alter "The Aleph"'s words, punctuation and style through adding his own text, and that this amounts to fraud and plagiarism according to Argentina's intellectual property law. Whatever the report's findings, this case will have implications that reach far beyond intellectual property lawyers and appeal courts in Argentina, spanning not just how we understand the Borgesian themes outlined above, but also how writers can engage with them and his considerable legacy in the modern day. Borges, viewing the Aleph for the first time, stated that "in that single gigantic instant I saw millions of acts both delightful and awful"; however, it is unlikely he expected this.

RESIDENCIA CORAZÓN

A PROJECT MADE BY ARTISTS FOR ARTISTS

by Suelen C. Martins

Located in vibrant La Plata, the capital of the state of Buenos Aires in Argentina, Residencia Corazón is a multicultural arts project which, for the past eight years, has welcomed artists from every discipline of the art world, to participate in an experience that will enhance their lives and their artistic work.

Home is where one feels comfortable enough to... draw on a wall! Walking through Residencia Corazón one walks past rooms that combine everyday life with the practice of making art – there are clothes strewn across the floor mixed with tubes of paint, works of art hidden behind plants in the garden, while the smell of the food from Mom's kitchen wafts through the house. The walls are painted with strong colours and are filled with the works of past residents. In essence, Residencia Corazón feels cosy and warm, like your favourite friend's house.

The project revolves around the idea of receiving artists from different parts of the world. They spend time living in the residence where they develop and present their ideas in the form of an exhibition, with the aim of creating an enriching cultural and artistic exchange. The residency was initiated in 2006 by Rodrigo Mirto, a visual artist, and Juan Pablo Ferrer, an arts and media worker, who were both in their mid-30s at the time. Mirto and Ferrer describe their decision to start the residency program as "the desire to do something different related to art. We wanted to bring the world to the city. We felt that the city and the cultural circuit [of La Plata] had stagnated."

Any big project requires a big effort, whether professional or personal, and both directors feel like each experience with a new artist is like a whole new beginning as each resident arrives with his or her own set of expectations, fears and ideas. As Mirto says: "The fact that it permanently changes is very mobilizing in all aspects." They accompany each resident from the time of their arrival and through his or her entire period of stay, including pre-production of the show and the presentation to the public. This results in a huge involvement. "You involve yourself emotionally with each artist beyond the professional. These are people who have broken up their everyday lives, and we need to make them feel good in every aspect and also to fulfil their expectations about our support of their artistic work. It can be really intense," adds Juan Pablo.

The artists generally arrive with the plan to stay for two months, and after this period most of them return to their homes, off on a trip around South America, or simply they decide to stay a little while longer! As Rachel Fuller, a writer from Australia, comments, "My experience at Residencia Corazón has been incredible. I originally came to the residency for two months in April and May of 2014. I then returned to Argentina in August and have now been back for a further four months – I love it that much!" At the moment Rachel shares the house with two other artists from Canada and Korea. She has almost become a family member as last month she assisted

Mirto and Ferrer in moving the residency to a new location. She adds, "For me, it has always been easy to make friends in La Plata. Every day I meet new people and the people of La Plata are open and genuinely interested in forming new relationships and friendships."

La Plata is a city with a great cultural scene. It hosts the National University of Fine Arts and also has an endless number of independent bands and musicians with some national and international recognition. As Rachel says, "I am constantly surprised by how often creative people in La Plata say that they really have no interest in being in the bigger 'creative capital' of Buenos Aires. Cultural life is very rich in La Plata." In the middle of all this artistic movement, Corazón tries to provide residents with a way to contribute and absorb some of what they experience in the city. In fact, many resident artists develop works which are highly influenced by the cultural characteristics of the city. "Often the city and the country is reflected in the artist's work. They live and absorb the culture of here," says Juan Pablo.

A project designed by artists for artists, in a country where the socio-economic context is always complicated, has not made running Residencia Corazón easy. There is a lack of financial government support for cultural initiatives in any sphere. As a result, the two founders of Corazón seek to provide a residency experience within a self-sustaining framework. At any one time there are two or three artists from around the world working at Residencia Corazón which seems to be a testament to the model they offer for both the local La Plata community and the artists who continue to arrive year after year.

It seems impossible to imagine bringing the world into a home but looking across the trajectory of Corazón over the past ten years it appears that Mirto and Ferrer have managed to mix a pinch of the Argentinean air with the cultural roots of each resident, resulting in exhibitions that capture the energy of this unique exchange. It is at once emotional and artistic and that has always have been the intention of Corazón. It is easy to imagine how big and full of life the world is in this house.

CUMBIA...

...AND THE DIFFICULT RELATIONSHIP BETWEEN ARGENTINA AND ITS LATIN IDENTITY

by Juan Data

Salsa never made it to Argentina. Of all the Spanish-speaking countries in the continent, Argentina is arguably the only one that managed to remain immune to the salsa explosion that originated in New York in the 70s and quickly became inseparable from Latino identity, worldwide.

Blame it on snobbism or Eurocentrism, but while everybody from Managua and Lima to Caracas were learning the swirling moves and falling under the spell of *salsa romántica*, Argentina's pop culture obsession was focused exclusively on Brit-pop, Italo-disco, new wave or whatever was hot that season on the Old World's radios and nightclubs. Historically Argentines, especially those from the big cities, felt like European expats that were accidentally born on the wrong side of the Atlantic and it was an intrinsic part of their national idiosyncrasy to reject any popular cultural expression emanating from anywhere else in the continent (with the only exception of Brazil, sometimes) for being professedly lowbrow and unsophisticated.

How can we then explain the cumbia phenomenon in Argentina? How did this tropical Latin genre manage to insert itself into the same hostile musical landscape that had proudly repelled salsa, merengue and all other genres commonly associated with tropical Latin America?

CUMBIA ENTERS THE PAMPAS

Cumbia was born in the Caribbean coast of Colombia and Panama, as a rural folk genre, associated with the carnival traditions of Afro-descendents. Later it moved to Medellín, where in the hands of the Discos Fuentes powerhouse it became the dominant pop music of Colombia throughout most of the 60s and until salsa and *vallenato* took over. From there, cumbia migrated to the rest of the continent, leaving behind its rural roots, to establish itself as the preferred blue collar party music everywhere from Los Angeles, California and Monterrey, Mexico to Santiago, Chile and Buenos Aires, Argentina.

When cumbia first arrived to Argentina in the early 60s, it was still very close to its Colombian rural roots. Accordion riffs led most songs, the *sombrero vueltiao* and traditional white get-ups were ubiquitous on album covers, lyrics abounded in references to fishermen and farm animals.

During this early period of cumbia's inception into Argentine culture, it wasn't yet associated with the working classes and the stigmas of being lowbrow or rustic that would follow the genre throughout the upcoming decades. In fact, Los Wawancó, one of the most successful artists during this embryonic phase, formed a multiracial and multicultural band of students at the University of Medicine. Cumbia was then accepted by many segments of the urban middle classes of Argentina, who saw the genre as part of a bigger continent-wide expression of folk and Latin roots music, that was considered progressive at the time.

In the following decade cumbia retreated away from the big cities and found its crowd in the rural areas and small towns of Argentina's provinces. During this period, cumbia started diversifying and seeking its own local identity: *cumbia norteña*, influenced by Peruvian *chicha* in the north-west, and the very successful *cumbia santafesina*, in the north-east region of the country, where cumbia got to mingle with local folk genres like *chamamé*.

It was also during the 70s, while the urban middle classes were distracted by the emerging *rock nacional* scene and the political *nueva trova* of the time, that cumbia started to become associated to the lower social classes of Argentina, without yet invoking the stigma of kitsch that would dominate during the decades that followed.

FLIRTING WITH THE MAINSTREAM

The return to democracy, in post-Falklands war Argentina, brought with it the promise of upward mobility and laissez-faire policies resulting in a massive migration towards the urban centres. Coming from rural backgrounds, small towns and poorer neighbouring nations, thousands of underprivileged people of predominantly indigenous or mestizo descent, converged in slums – locally called *villas* – settled in the surroundings of every major urban centre. With them, they brought cumbia back to the big city.

Villas grew exponentially during and after the 80s, and cumbia was the default soundtrack of villa life. This cumbia, however, had little in common with the folksy roots of its predecessor's. Long gone were the Colombian hats, the accordion had been replaced by the synth and melodramatic lyrics about love lost and not-so-subtle double-entendres substituted fishermen stories once and for all. Thus, cumbia became synonymous with kitsch. Bands, dressed in sequin-studded matching outfits, played it on late night TV shows and on radio stations that targeted the working classes, while the middle class youth ignored the phenomenon completely and consumed a strict diet of London-approved sounds.

The first paradigm shift happened right at the end of that decade. In 1989 Menem was elected president of Argentina and brought with him populist ideals and aesthetics that permeated through all levels of society. The previously state-controlled TV stations got privatized and, overnight, cumbia crossed over to the mainstream when prime time TV shows started booking tropical artists as headliners. The conservative, older,

Eurocentric elites were expectably horrified and accused the media of 'levelling down' the country's culture. Still, cumbia quickly became a massive boom amongst the youth. Even the most exclusive nightclubs that appealed only to the predominantly white upper classes, started mixing cumbia into their playlists that summer, and the affluent dancers embraced it 'ironically' in the safety of these venues where the authentic cumbia crowd were only allowed in as janitorial service.

From that moment on cumbia would become established in the average Argentine sonic menu as standard, disposable party music. This, of course, didn't mean cumbia was respected as a legitimate art form. Cumbia had indeed infiltrated the mainstream, but only as a joke. Music critics didn't take the genre seriously and the *rock nacional* establishment saw it as a threat or, at best, disregarded it completely. Cumbia was just fun, cheaply produced music for maids and bus drivers to consume. Even when they did dance to it 'ironically' at parties and nightclubs, the predominantly white Eurocentric youth of Argentina's middle class didn't purchase cumbia albums, nor did they attend live cumbia shows. The social divide between the real cumbia crowd and the casual upper class listener was still very rigid.

THE ATTACK OF THE CLONES

Once cumbia broke into the mainstream in the late 80s, it never left. Soon it had afternoon-long TV shows dedicated to it every weekend. There were radio stations spinning cumbia 24/7 and cumbia stars were even getting coverage by the gossip magazines. Cumbia was big business, but the big business was mostly controlled by an oligopoly of two record labels and a handful of producers that ran it all: the TV shows, the radio stations and, more importantly, the cumbia nightclubs, known locally as *bailantas*. Under the control of this oligopoly, cumbia in the 90s became overtly commercial, with new gimmick-centric, assembly-line groups introduced to the masses every week, and innumerable clones of every mildly successful gimmick saturating the market shortly after.

For example, for a while during the mid-90s, there was a popularity peak of manufactured cumbia boy bands, where all the members were selected through casting, more based on their looks than their talent. Long hair was mandatory, choreographed dance-steps and matching outfits were also, still, commonplace.

On a typical weekend night, these cloned cumbia bands, would tour multiple *bailantas*, doing short lip-synch performances with unplugged instruments (the keytar, now an iconic instrument forever associated with Argentine cumbia, became prevalent during this period because it allowed 'musicians' to dance choreographed steps while 'playing').

Of course there were some exceptions to the rule and a handful of legitimate cumbia artists approached the genre with respect and penned some memorable compositions (i.e. Antonio Ríos), but the 90s will forever be remembered as the era of manufactured cumbia.

While none of this contributed to the genre earning any respect, it was during those years that select rock bands began flirting with cumbia and mixing it into their repertoires, sometimes achieving more commercial success than the actual cumbia bands themselves, simply because rocker's cred gave them access to a sector of the hermetic music media that otherwise shunned cumbia.

THE RISE OF CUMBIA VILLERA

The next big cultural revolution took place at the end of the decade, with the rise of what would be labelled *cumbia villera*. Coinciding with the fall of Menem and, with him, the neo-liberal politics that obliterated the country's industry, the former working class became the unemployed class that still listened to cumbia but didn't identify with the genre's corny lyrics anymore. *Cumbia villera* came into the scene to supply a dormant demand for songs that really reflected what villa dwellers were experiencing in their own day-to-day lives. It was a drastic change of tone, like going from glossy Motown soul to hard-core gangsta rap with no stops in between.

Now completely detached from its Caribbean rural roots, *cumbia villera* borrowed inspiration from *cumbia norteña*, Mexican *cumbia sonidera*, reggae, reggaeton, *rock barrial* and football hooligan subculture and came up with a totally new way of making cumbia that was 100% authentically Argentine. Where cumbia in the 90s was dominated by pretty-face boys in matching outfits, *cumbia villera* artists looked and dressed like your everyday street kid. Grit replaced fake glamour and double-entendres disappeared to make room for in-your-face explicit lyrics about crime, sex and drug abuse. It could be argued that *cumbia villera* was the first pop cultural expression of racial and class pride for the oppressed Argentine mestizo people.

The economic collapse that hit Argentina in 2001 did nothing but help propel *cumbia villera* to the forefront. For the first time, Argentine cumbia became the focus of interest of journalists and sociologists around the world. The established labels and producers that controlled the genre saw it as another gimmick and manufactured a bunch of *cumbia villera* clones to saturate the market, but the original, legit *cumbia villera* artists (i.e., Pablo Lescano's Damas Gratis) managed to maintain a level of independence and control over their catalogue, which allowed them, in turn, to earn the respect of many within the decaying *rock nacional* establishment.

Cumbia villera enjoyed peak popularity during the first three years of the new millennium, followed by a backlash when the federal communications agency implemented a new law that limited the broadcasting of the genre in mainstream media due to foul language. By then, however, the innocence was forever lost and cumbia would never go back to what it used to be.

The economic crisis had another interesting effect: prompted by the circumstances, middle class Argentines, to a certain extent, left behind some of their exceptionalism and realized they were, after all, another country in Latin America. Inspired in part

by this new paradigm, a new breed of middle class Argentine musicians, many of them coming from the electronic music, hip-hop and dub scenes, started looking inward for inspiration. Instead of focusing so much on replicating the latest European trends, they started experimenting with re-contextualized, sample-based cumbia and other native Latin sounds, thus giving birth to *ñu-cumbia*.

The crisis also made Argentina temporarily affordable as a destination for first-world tourism and, all of a sudden, the streets of Buenos Aires became crowded with English-speaking foreigners fascinated by the underground scene of *ñu-cumbia* (also referred to as *cumbia digital*), which became the 'it' thing of the season for hipsters, both sides of the Atlantic.

Ñu-cumbia, however, never fully crossed to the mainstream in its birthplace. It summoned tons of media attention and praise from critics and bloggers worldwide, but in Argentina it was still considered a miniscule underground scene that appealed mainly to expats searching for the exotic South American experience in a safe environment. Nevertheless, it contributed in bridging the gap between social classes and making cumbia a lot more inclusive.

CUMBIA'S FINAL FRONTIER?

The latest stage in Argentine cumbia's evolution is what some are calling *rugbier cumbia*, or *cumbia cheta* (*cheta* meaning snob or rich). Basically, this is cumbia by white kids from affluent backgrounds and private school education (rugby is the preferred sport of elitist educational establishments in Argentina, hence the name) that were born and raised in an environment where cumbia was always in the mainstream and came of age in an era where there were no more clear divisions between high and low culture.

Accused by many of cultural appropriation, these rich kids approached cumbia from a fresh perspective, freed of the long-held stigmas of the genre, they simply adopted the contagious cumbia rhythm and its basic instrumentation to make edgeless but catchy pop songs. At first glance one might be sceptical and dismiss them as yet another gimmick manufactured by a record producer with acute commercial aim, however when interviewed, most of these kids claim they naturally arrived to cumbia on their own and while they agree they may not be the genre's archetypal consumers, they all grew up listening and singing along to the latest cumbia hits at social gatherings. Unlike previous generations, their approach to cumbia is completely irony-free.

EL MAESTRO

While the phenomenon is not strictly Argentine (most of the *rugbier cumbia* artists hail from Uruguay, actually), it became a massive success in recent years, taking over the local pop charts during the summer of 2016. Ultimately, *rugbier cumbia* seems like the aesthetic nemesis of *cumbia villera*. Band members typically look like clean-cut, preppy, frat boys and in most cases they include a female vocalist (fair-skinned, blonde and blue eyed, preferably) in front.

It may be yet another passing fad and Argentine cumbia might still evolve into something else next summer, or the following. One thing is for sure, the country that once rejected all tropical music, has finally accepted cumbia as one of its autochthonous forms of popular expression and cumbia in Argentina is here to stay, for good.

Three of the best-selling albums in Argentine cumbia history: Antonio Rios - *El Maestro* (1996), Gilda - *Corazón Valiente* (1995) and Pibes Chorros - *Arriba Las Manos* (2001)

BETTY CONFETTI'S ROMANTIC CUMBIA CONJUNTO

An unlikely ambassador for Argentine cumbia, Betty Confetti grew up in Portsmouth before moving to Berlin, falling in love with an Argentine and then finding herself living in Buenos Aires, which is where she's stayed. As well as playing in the post-punk band Las Kellies she started a musical solo project which, after she became infatuated with cumbia, morphed into a group called Betty Confetti y su Conjunto Tropical. In the past seven years they've become a fixture of Buenos Aires' live music scene, releasing one album and a number of EPs. So, how did a girl from the south coast of England end up starting a cumbia group in Argentina?

What first got you interested in cumbia?

My first encounter with cumbia was when I got here in 2005, hearing that unmistakable rhythm pumping from cars on the street, and automatically being hip-shaken along the pavement. It took me years to get into it, as my friends were more into The Ramones and Pink Floyd; there was a definite disdain for popular cumbia. It wasn't until friends made me listen to Gilda (a local popular 'saint') and the likes of Los Mirlos and Juaneco y Su Combo of the Peruvian *chicha* set, that I became increasingly obsessed with the genre, and I delved into this, for me, new musical language. Indie, rock, noise... it all seemed mundane at this point. There's a lot of local variety in cumbia from all over the continent. At first Gilda's anthem "No Me Arrepiento de Este Amor" set me off, along with "Ya Se Ha Muerto Mi Abuelo" by Juaneco y Su Combo. I was also given an album by *cumbia villera* greats Pibes Chorros, and there was a song on there called "Pokemon" which I found truly offensive and misogynist, but it kept me listening. Much later on I discovered the original *cumbiamberos* of Colombia, such as Aniceto Molina.

What's the scene like for cumbia in Buenos Aires?

The scene has changed so much since I started getting into it. I recall taking some intrigued European friends to dance cumbia in the Paraguayan club Mburukuyá in (ill-advised for tourists) Constitución, and we were told by the taxi driver to take a knife with us and never look at anyone in the club. It was a genre 'just for the lower classes'. I'd get criticized by strangers for playing a style of music that 'has no content' and is 'just about drugs and condoning crime'. Nowadays there is the *cumbia cheta* (posh cumbia) movement, so that the kind of venues that previously only put on indie/rock/alternative nights are filling up with cumbia bands from all kinds of backgrounds.

We've played with some great *cumbia villera* bands, but would love to collaborate with them more. Mala Fama and Damas Gratis are big references for newer songs, those *villeros* that had huge success around the 2001 economic crisis, and write great social poetry using the local slang, too close to the bone, and only just starting to be recognized as 'culture' nowadays. Everyone knows the lyrics!

Paul Cheese by Sebastian Litmanovich

FROM 'REBELDE' TO 'TONTOS'

RETRACING THE FOOTSTEPS OF EXPERIMENTAL ARGENTINE ROCK

by Alan Courtis

translated by Alexandra Nataf

For a generation in Argentina, rock music was one of the most significant voices. Although experimentation was never in itself a highly-valued quality in this field, consciously or not, the rock music that emerged in Argentina during the 60s and 70s had a lot to offer in that respect. Experimental rock in Argentina avoided established models and reformulated creative structures through which unique sounds emerged, often despite the rejection and incomprehension of the audience and the critics. This article follows the footsteps of experimental rock in Argentina, discussing music that was 'experimental' considering its historical and social context at the time.

BEGINNINGS: BETWEEN UNCONSCIOUSNESS AND INTUITION (1966-1969)

It is usually thought that Argentinean rock, at least in its origins, had a vital quota of experimentation. Wanting to assimilate the huge wave of Anglo-Saxon music and its guitar, bass and drums format, then adjust it with local characteristics, was not an easy task.

At first, the simple fact of writing and singing rock 'in castellano', or more precisely 'in Argentine', was a statement and a sign of taking risks. At first it was not considered a good idea by many producers to sing in Spanish, and if it had not been for the early, and massive, hit of "La Balsa" in 1967, history would probably have been quite different.

Many agree that *rock nacional* (the common term in Argentine for rock specifically from their country) started in the 1960s with Los Beatnicks. Founded by Moris, Pajarito Zaguri and Javier Martinez in Villa Gesell, they only released one single, "Rebelde" (1966) which features traces of experimentation (though probably not intended). It is considered the first recorded national rock track and contains passages of 'vocal guitar' in which Zaguri imitates the sound of a distorted electric guitar with his mouth; he used this technique again in "El Soldado", a track that was never released. It was surely a clever idea given the lack of equipment, but it was still an early form of experimentation. This predilection for pushing limits was confirmed later on with a performance they gave in their truck while driving around the city with a handwritten sign in their hands to promote their single. They finished off the performance by jumping in a fountain. By which time the police had intervened to put an end to the scandal.

Known as Tango, Tanguito or Ramsés VII (after the Egyptian Pharaoh), José Alberto Iglesias ended up becoming a legend following his premature and suspicious death on a railway. His eccentric influence was significant when it came to creating a proper *castellano* voice in rock as well as inventing a distinctive style of poetic lyrics based on enigmatic metaphors. Although his only album, released post-mortem, is recorded rustically, it rawly exposes Tango's talent as a troubadour of excess. More than a studio album, it sounds like something that could have been sung in the public environs of Plaza Francia's sandbox [a popular public space in Buenos Aires] as dawn approached. Not only did he release songs that were as personal as his own myth but he also produced an incredible amount of work using vocal improvisations, which seem to have been overlooked at the time. What Tango did intuitively by 'imitating trumpets' using his voice and making noises that were on the verge of being out-of-tune, could be seen as a form of 'mouth music' or 'sound poetry'.

We can find some experimentation in the pioneering 'psychedelic beat' of Los Gatos ("Una Nube en Tu Vida") or in Manal's *'porteño'* blues ("Avellaneda Blues"), however what sticks out in the experimental field amongst the founding Argentinean rock bands is Almendra. Spinetta Molinari, Del Guercio and Garcia's band were a key element in progressing Argentine rock music. What did they sound like? It's difficult to say, possibly a mixture between the Beatles and Hendrix, with a celestial singer and a certain tango-inspired atmosphere. However what is to be sure of is that, although this may sound terribly redundant, Almendra sounds like Almendra. On one hand, they introduced a lyrical quality that was until then rarely heard in songs, a mixture of sophisticated surrealism with lyrics related to *porteño* life. On the other hand, they challenged formal conventions through the individuality of their songs and the band's sound as well as the length of the songs. This was made very clear on their double album (known as *Almendra II* or simply 'Almendra's double album') which was conceived as a rock opera about 'man's inner search', but ended up being inconclusive and unclassifiable. The development and length of the tracks seemed to be prioritizing creativity over commerciality, allowing improvisation to have a prestigious place within their sound. This is clear on the 14-minute-long "Agnus Dei", the closest to an anti-hit they ever wrote, in which they push the tonal limits of electric improvisation. What made them interesting was their ability to combine songs that were popular on the radio ("Muchacha Ojos de Papel") with tracks that are more difficult to listen to such as "Vine al Planeta" (from the album *En Vivo en Teatro del Globo 69*).

During these early days Moris has to be mentioned because of his innovative approach to songwriting on songs like "Escúchame Entre el Ruido" and "De Nada Sirve". We also can't forget Miguel Abuelo and his first band Los Abuelos de la Nada, a band that reached the high spheres of local psychedelia. Their second single, featuring "Diana Diavaga" and "Tema en Flú Sobre el Planeta", combined the 'beat' sound with strings, screaming and sound effects that included bells and explosions. Their desire to change the song structures of the time is clear in the concepts behind their songs and lyrics, as well as their vocals and instrumentation. All the singles released by Abuelo right up to 1970 on their label Mandioca had this same profile; "Hoy Seremos Campesinos" stands out for its remarkable orchestral arrangements, harmonic dissonances and processed voices which made it a stand-out album with its own experimental identity, far from foreign models.

HARD ROCK: ELECTRIC THINKING

After more than a generation of existence, renovating and expanding itself, rock music made it to new frontiers by the late 60s and on into the 70s. The political instability of the time and the hostility of ferocious repression (during and between dictatorships) are factors that cannot be overlooked and that undeniably conditioned all the records of the time. Given these events – already very different from what was in the 'first world' – local rock radicalized itself in its aesthetical and ethical quest.

In that sense, La Pesada was an important transitional bridge between the first bands and what came next. Led by Billy Bond, a talented producer, the band gathered together a legion of musicians that rotated in recording and playing live. With their anti-establishment position, their incredible energy, creativity and sense of humour, they embodied the heaviest branch of rock as well as a ferocious social criticism. Their first productions are proof of that combination, for example in the track "Verdes Prados"'s phrasing, in "Buen Dia Señor Presidente"'s intense bridge (from their first album), or in the collective catharsis of "Que Descanses en Paz" from their second LP. If you had to name an album of which the vocation was to take rock music to the edge of being recognisable, few recordings have gone as far as *Tontos (Operita)*. It was without a doubt one of the most explicit attempts to experiment: an album without songs, an integral conceptual piece. In this sound collage that revolves around the composition in situ of the track "Tontos", layers of sound coming from different sources constantly erupt, bringing concrete music techniques to its wildest edge. The piece is completed with artwork whose provocative naïvety contrasts with allusions to an incident at their Luna Park show, when due to confrontation with police the place was practically destroyed by part of the audience [the album includes the date of the incident along with a cross (20th October 1972 †), and extensively uses 'blood red']. This album, published by the label Music Hall in 1972, is probably one of the most experimental pieces in the history of Argentinean music.

La Pesada was also a platform to release solo albums from its members. In *Jorge Pinchevsky, Su Violín Mágico y La Pesada*, the search revolved around the sound of the violin. Coming from a classical training, Pinchevsky made sure to decontextualize it, transposing it to the extreme rock templates of the time. This very original mixture is obvious in songs such as "La Maravillosa Marta y la Fuerza de las Cosas" or "Parte de Baile para Grupos y Solistas" and this results in gaudy solos, on the edge of tonal minimalism, which dominate the development of the album.

Pinchesvky then emigrated to Europe where he ended up playing live with one of the pioneering bands of space rock, Gong, with whom he recorded the album *Shamal*. Meanwhile, Kubero Díaz was a guitarist for La Cofradía de la Flor Solar, a band and an artistic community of La Plata, whose experimental vocation was certified by their multimedia show "La Mezcladora de Cemento", which they presented at the Instituto Di Tella in 1968. La Cofradía also left behind a finished album and a single, in which they explore different atmospheres through electric guitar sounds. After playing in Billy Bond's band for many years, in 1976 Díaz recorded his first and only solo album to date, *Kubero Dìaz y la Pesada*. The LP, nowadays valued by collectors, not only shows his talents as a guitarist but also various moments of his creative journey in songs such as "Polvo he de Sacudir" or in "Spirtrepus", an odd track with processed keyboards and voices. In 1972 Claudio Gabis recorded his first album with the second incarnation of La Pesada. On *Claudio Gabis y La Pesada*, he picks up his musical roots and takes them in different directions: going towards 'rock alterado' (altered rock) in some ("Fiebre de la Ruta") and instrumental folk in others ("El Viaje de Lord Dunsany"). However, as had already occurred in his album *Buenos Aires Blues*, the ex-Manal man goes back to his principal genre in "Blues del Terror Azul", in which he uses a typical blues structure infested with dissonant sounds and effects that take him to a new level of estrangement. The lyrics make obvious allusions to the repression already present in those days and that would end up being one of the most ferocious dictatorships.

Three fundamental bands emerged from Almendra's split: Spinetta formed Pescado Rabioso, while Molinari did likewise with Color Humano, and Del Güercio and García formed Aquelarre. These three bands represent a step forward towards hard rock but with an imaginative focus that extended the musical forms, yet with distinct nuances in each case.

In Pescado Rabioso, while the sources of inspiration might be identifiable (from Led Zeppelin to Rimbaud) the final result is too personal to put it in a box. In fact, despite having been Spinetta's most 'rocking' band, it seems that in *Pescado 2* there is a place for all types of music: from his modified vocals in "Panadera Ensoñado" to alienated passages in "Viajero Naciendo", from the trivial sections of "Madreselva" to the minimalist drive of "Peteribí", from the odd melody of "Corto" to the mini-rock-opera orchestrations of "Aguas Claras de Olimpos". With *Artaud*, an album Pescado Rabioso is given credit for but which is actually by Spinetta as a soloist, the surrealism and song format reach one of the highest points of national rock. Right from the cover, with its irregular format, it's an album that sticks out from convention, yet with results so particular that it ended up being a classic. The album offers songs such as "Cementerio Club", "Bajan" and "Cantata de Puentes Amarillos" with a great delicacy in their writing, harmonies and melodies; however the experimental highlights are "Por", a song based on free grammatical association, the final collage of "La Sed Verdadera" and "A Starosta, el Idiota" and its bridge full of special effects like piano clusters, tapes played backwards, sobbing and even primitive samples from the Beatles. Although it has been less exposed, it is impossible to ignore Spinetta's preceding album called *La Búsqueda de la Estrella* (edited again as *Spinettalandia y Sus Amigos* later on) which is, perhaps, his weirdest piece. With a high degree of improvisation, songs that oscillate between acid folk ("Ni Cuenta te Das"), an ethnic trip ("Estrella") and rock on its way to destruction ("Altercación de Tiempo") appear on this album.

In the case of Color Humano, the power-trio led by Edelmiro Molinari, the particular way he sings, the lyrics and structure of the songs as well as the use of the electric guitar are innovations in themselves. It is difficult to know where Molinari's personal 'spoken' singing style comes from – it can be heard on songs like "Sílbame Oh! Cabeza" and "Sangre del Sol". The lyrics show the continuation of his previous quest with Almendra but with a more cryptic poetry that can be seen in passages such as "camino a campos / de riquezas más extrañas / ya no existe final/la alborada tupida recubrió / cicatrices de mil campañas / en las cosas de otras gentes / y un idioma brutal / destelló con campanas y cuerdas" ("on the way to fields / of strange wealth / it has no end / the dense covered dawn / scars from thousand of campaigns / across other peoples' things / and a brutal language / flashing with bells and strings"). With a remarkable contribution from Rafanelli on the bass and Moro (or Lebón) on the drums, the structures of pieces like "Larga Vida al Sol" or "El Hachazo" show complexity in the production but principally a psychedelic sonority with lots of space left for improvisation and melodic and harmonic experimentation, as in "Humanoides" or in "A Través de los Inviernos".

Molinari always had a particular guitar sound and unmistakable phrasing which included harmonics, vibratos and curious sounds extracted from the bridge of his instrument. In that sense, sometimes his guitar becomes unrecognizable, as is the case in the intense solos of "Las Historias que Tengo" and "Va a Salir un Lugar", which guarantee him a privileged seat amongst the pioneering electric guitar experimenters of Argentina.

In Aquelarre there is also a sense of exploration though they are more focused on the general conception of the compositions: the idea seems to be to extend the song format to achieve long 'chamber music pieces' of great instrumental development where melodies appear and fade out with great distress. With the protagonism fairly distributed: several vocalists, a solid rhythmic base (Del Güercio-García) added to which are González Neira's keyboards and Starc's rock touch, the band has since the beginning relied on collective composition. This gave them a very organic character which led to them progressively searching for great subtlety while still conserving a potent side; guaranteeing them a singular identity. One of the most interesting elements was their renovation of song forms, as if certain formalities of the genre were already exhausted; they tried to avoid foreseeable choruses and work on melodies with rhythmical irregularities and harmonic complexities. Through their solid compositions they succeeded in making them hits ("Violencia en el Parque"). They also got strong results because of their use of textures and atmosphere; "Canto", "Yo Seré el Animal, Tú Serás Mi Dueño" or "Brumas en la Bruma" are good examples.

Partly because of his exile to France, Miguel Abuelo recorded only one album that was close to hard rock. *Miguel Abuelo et Nada* is a cult album that stands out because of its concept and production, as well as the careful compositions, poetic lyrics, and inimitable vocal style that guarantees Abuelo a certain originality resistant to the passing of time. The album features different atmospheres that alternate in usual and clever ways ("Tirando Piedras al Río", "Estoy Aquí Parado, Sentado y Acostado"). The production was very adventurous: processed vocals, effects, panning, a sound palette amplified through electric and acoustic sounds, as well as the inclusion of a cello which incorporated classical (and medieval) touches in counterpoint to Daniel Sbarra's potent guitar. And in order to deepen his explorative adventure, Edgardo Cantón, Horacio Vaggione and Gustavo Kerestesachi collaborated with them to create sound effects (those who worked in Pierre Schaeffer's studio) on a song that reaches disturbing climaxes ("El Muelle"). What first seemed like a mere support between people in exile, ended up being the only collaboration between famous figures of electro-acoustic and rock music that ever happened in Argentinean music.

Other bands to consider are Piel de Pueblo, Pajarito Zaguri, Willy Pedemonte, Nacho Smilari and Carlos Calabró's band. Their album *Rock de las Heridas* is also composed of a certain degree of experimentation, especially in "La Tierra en 998 Pedazos", made oddly original by weird keyboard sounds and Pedemonte's surrealist lyrics. Pedemonte would later have an important role in the recording of *Miguel Cantilo y Grupo Sur*, probably Cantilo's closest attempt at heavy rock. It was recorded in El Bolsón with a potent sound that

Right: Almendra - *II* (1970); Arco Iris - *Sudamerica O El Regreso A La Aurora* (1972); Ave Rock - *Ave Rock* (1974)

reaches instrumental abandon, and politically-engaged lyrics ("El Mito del Regreso", "Las Imágenes que Ves Entre Las Nubes") that lead into extreme singing and screaming. On the other hand, Smilari and Calabró formed the band Cuero with Enrique Maslloren. Their first album *Tiempo Después* offers a profound psychedelic experience noticeable in the flow of vocals, drums and guitars coming in at the higher peaks of intensity, as in the unexpected finale of "Paula Acurrucada en un Color". In this field even some work by Pappo's Blues can be considered as experimentation in hard rock music, especially on their album *Triángulo*, which showcases their famous guitar player working alongside hermetic lyrics and tapes played backwards ("Mírese Adentro"), and instrumental passages remote from established structures ("Hubo Distancias en un Curioso Baile Matinal Parte II"), even generating one unclassifiable piece "El Buzo".

HYBRIDIZATION: CROSS-OVER GENRES AND CULTURES

Another important axis of the experimental development of these years was centred around the combination of musical genres of different traditions. The band that explored that path before anyone else was Arco Iris, whose leader was Gustavo Santaolalla – already in the 60s cross-overs between rock and folk music were happening. On their first album, recorded in 1969, we can hear a mixture of screeching electric guitars and acoustic instruments playing typical folkloric rhythms. Far from the conservatism of mainstream folklore festivals like Cosquín [one of Argentina's most important folk festivals], they achieved a musical melting-pot which ended up being very innovative: there were pieces full of effects and lyrics far from realism, like "Tiempo" or "Canción de Cuna para un Niño Cosmonauta". Arco Iris continued their activities for several years, making albums such as the rock-opera *Sudamérica: el Regreso de la Aurora* and the double album *Agitor Lucens V*, a conceptual piece that investigated the connections between extraterrestrial existence and pre-Columbian cultures. Other artists tried to mix folkloric music with their rock influences, such as Huinca (Litto Nebia's parallel project), Magma (from Paraná), Contraluz and Gabriela. Definitely worth mentioning are Los Jaivas' (originally from Chile) who recorded two albums during their stay in Argentina. On both albums *Los Jaivas* and *Canción del Sur*, the brothers Parra and Gato Alquinta show their talent through long compositions and instrumental improvisations in which native (*trutrucas, tarkas, zampoñas, charango*, etc.) and electric (guitar, bass and even synthesizers) instruments mix together with considerable ease and coherence. It is enough to listen to "Tarka y Ocarina", "Canción del Sur-co" or "Danza" to appreciate this particular mixture that, without losing themselves in their experimentation, made them – alongside the Peruvians El Polen, Wara in Bolivia and Genesis in Colombia – one of the emblematic bands of the popular Latin American music and rock crossovers.

Another genre where musical crossovers are well accepted is jazz music. It is possible to find diverse projects that mixed jazz elements with rock. The pioneer was guitarist Oscar Alemán, a musician capable of tackling any musical genre, which he had already done in the 50s when he released swing versions of "Rock Alrededor del Reloj" and "Bailando el Rock 'n' Roll". Later on, bands like Fe, Alma y Vida (who had in their stable formation a sax and trumpet) and Santa y Clarificación (the band of Rodolfo Alchourrón, who also created orchestral arrangements for Almendra, Miguel Abuelo, Nebbia and Aquelarre), appeared. Quinteplus was an ensemble whose musicians came from jazz but got close to rock and funk music with a musical formation that included a piano and traditional jazz wind instruments as well as drums, bass, electric guitar and keyboards, which for the time was extremely innovative. Gato Barbieri was another artist that crossed over in that field. He conducted several ensembles with electric touches, integrating diverse genres. The crossover album of Ara Tokatlián (of Arco Iris) and the remembered pianist Enrique 'Mono' Villegas's is well worth mentioning. On *Inspiración*, using piano, wind instruments and double bass formation, they go from compositions full of climaxes to free jazz without ever stopping. In this regard, the group Sintesis on their homonymous instrumental album deliver a very special blend of jazz, blues and classical with some tango flavour due to a unique line-up that combines the traditional power-rock-trio with guests playing saxophones, clarinet, flute and violin.

Also Invisible, one of the most singular bands that national rock has created, also used jazz elements but integrated them progressively with hard rock and Spinetta's usual lyrical poetry. With Pomo and Machi in charge of the instrumental foundations, they made a transition to experimental language on their albums *Invisible* and *Durazno Sangrando*, as well as on their singles. However on their last album, *El Jardín de los Presentes*, the accordion of Juan José Mosalini was added, enabling them to include some refined tango ambiences. Spinetta had always suggested an influence of tango, and that finally materialized on that album, creating a hit out of this fusion of genres on "Los Libros de la Buena Memoria". It is worth mentioning that the guitar player Tomás Gubitsch that appeared on that album, later joined Ástor Piazzolla's band (as Osvaldo Caló from Ave Rock also did) until their political beliefs differed too much and they split. During that brief period of flirting with rock music, Piazzolla endorsed bands such as Alas, that ended up using three accordions when playing live. This band is quite particular because on their albums (*Alas* and *Pinta Tu Aldea*) they created a highly abstract fusion that included folklore, *música ciudadana* [urban music], progessive symphonic music and 'Kosmische Musik'.

Going back to tango, Rodolfo Mederos and Generación Cero's albums are to be taken into account, as well as other artists that tried to tackle the genre with electric instrumentation (not surprisingly Gubitsch appears here too), which some had no hesitation in christening 'rock tango'. Anyway, tango always had a natural attraction for electric guitars, such as with Ubaldo de Lío or in certain guitar excursions like those of Oscar López Ruiz and Horacio Malvicino. But one of the first and the most daring experiments in this field was Eduardo Rovira's album *Sónico*. Salvador Drucker (electric guitar), Néstor Mendy (amplified double bass) and Rovira himself (who bordered on atonality at times, even putting a pedal effect on his accordion) participated in this album's recording in 1968. It is without a doubt one of the most significant attempts to reinvigorate the traditional language of tango in history.

Returning to the specific rocker's sphere, several bands made crossovers and the results are mitigated. For example in 1977, Charly García made "Hipercandombe" with La

Máquina de Hacer Pájaros, which was a curious crossover using *candombe* rhythms, progressive rock and an electric sound full of synths, tango touches recalling Piazzolla and criticism against the dictatorship. In the case of Bubu, his only album *Anabelas* of 1978 exposes a complex framework situated somewhere between chamber music, progressive rock, contemporary classical music and free jazz which had little precedent in the country. With influences as varied as Stravinsky, King Crimson, Messiaen and Zappa, while still maintaining an inventive personality, they tried to extend national rock's horizons. It is one of the only projects of the kind in this time period. Their closeness to classical traditions is noticeable in the careful use of the ensemble's sound palette, however this did not make them lose strength, as their recordings feature moments of exuberant energy. During that time period, another band that drew its inspiration from classical music was the collective M.I.A.. They managed to distance themselves from the predictability of symphonic rock, as in "Archipiélagos de Güernaclara". Their principal innovation was at an organisational level, when they founded a pioneering independent cooperative. From Tucumán, another independent group were Redd, who made an interesting progressive synthesis. They wrote songs such as "Reyes en Guerra" or the song that gave its name to their first album, "Tristes Noticias del Imperio", that can be characterised by their changing structures, solid instrumental work and the contribution of several synthesizers. It also seems necessary to mention the band Ave Rock that had already, years before, in 1974, made recordings with complex irregular passages and carefully-crafted production. This unique combination of progressive rock with classical touches also included potent moments of garage rock. Their first album, one of the most accomplished in this area, shows a fine work of contrast ("Ausencia") between climaxes and melodies ("Déjenme Seguir"), of which there is a long collective piece that stands out entitled "Viva Bélgica".

MISCELLANEOUS EXPERIMENTS: RESCUE AND REVALUATION

In a context like the Argentine one, so inefficient at collecting and conserving our music, there is still much more to investigate in terms of experimentation. Adding to this is the fact that several projects may well be forgotten about – some of those mentioned are already out-of-print or were never published in the first place. In terms of these bands, close to extinction, there are a number that are significant enough to be mentioned here as examples.

One of these is El Sonido de Hillber, a band that officially only realeased one single in 1970. They were the first band to play with a string quartet and although their attempt was not particularly successful, they managed to create an interesting balance between the band and strings. Another remarkable discovery is the odd "Días Después" that concludes the album *Cuando Brille el Tiempo* by Montes, throughout which Jorge Montes creates unheard of and indescribable sounds with his guitar.

On the other hand, the band Orion's Beethoven, who were the first band to use processed voices and diverse effects, achieved a psychedelic hard rock sound with obscure harmonies and epic lyrics. On their first album, *Superángel*, between other eccentricities,

SOUNDS AND COLOURS ARGENTINA

is included a rock version of Schubert's "8th Symphony in B Minor". Another anomaly is *Erótica*, the hilarious album that Billy Bond, with members of La Pesada, produced for Jorgelina Aranda, which oscillates between lounge music and B movie soundtracks.

On *Sin Tiempo ni Espacio* by Los Barrocos there is a small experimental song entitled "Historia de una Confabulación Destinada a Fracasar" that introduces an abundant sound exploration through guitars that cover up the constant eruption of deranged sharp violins. Carola (Cutaia), before relasing her LP *Damas Negras*, published a surprising single (with the help of her husband and friends) with a very peculiar song called "Eva Estirpe Terrena".

Originally from Santa Fe, Agnus was an ensemble with remarkable female participation whose name was inspired by the previously mentioned song by Almendra. They took the psychedelic adventure quite far in their only released work *Pinturas y Expresiones*. Another album worth mentioning is the unclassifiable *Que Estan Celebrandro los Hombres* by Nono Belvis and Kike Sanzol (from M.I.A.) in which improvisation is the principal tool to connect different sound explorations.

Unfortunately some projects and artists with an interest in experimentation never managed to publish their pieces officially, as is the case for OM, La Pequeña Banda de Tricupa (de Tucumán), Igoagrio y las Crestas del Extrangulo (de Trenque Lauquen), Supermoco, La Brujutrampa, Trigémino, Aschabel, Raúl Roca and Tarso Calmo.

CONCLUSIONS

As we have seen, rock music contributed to the experimental music canon a lot, however it cannot be seen as an organic whole but more as an expansive range of diverse experiences which, quite often, were actually opposed to each other. Following these experimental times, it seems pertinent to ask where one can now find experimentation in rock music.

During the 80s experimental rock remained underground, before emerging when democracy arrived and new technologies appeared. In the 90s, it had to resist the intense 'marketing' of the MTV era and survive in ever more compressed spaces. Nowadays, it is possible that some of these experimental seeds remain and it could be that they will be taken over by new generations, although probably not through commercial chains. It is all about waiting for changes in the counter-culture, and any change can be a step forward. In any case, changes have to be analysed, as behind every positive advance, be it contextual or technological, there are always new forms of control. Although the panorama is not very encouraging, new experimental forms can and will be found in the coming decades. And I hope that something from these early years will survive and not end up destructed by this marketing machinery which only uses it as an excuse to sell fizzy drinks.

THE MUSIC SCENE IN LA PLATA

Ariel Valeri is a journalist and photographer from General Roca who has made La Plata is home for the best part of the last 20 years. For the past 13 years of those he has been working FM Universidad, the most important rock station in the city, as well as writing about and photographing the local music scene. There are few better people to speak to in order to find out what's happening in La Plata.

How would you describe the music scene in La Plata? What are the most prominent scenes (rock, pop, electronic, etc.)?

La Plata has several scenes, but all on a small scale. It is a city that does not even have one million inhabitants and rock, generally speaking, is not the most popular genre for a lot of youngsters. Perhaps cumbia pop today dominates almost everything, albeit from a more commercial aspect. *Platense rock* remains on the margins though occasionally a band makes it outside of the city, the latest to do which is El Mato A Un Policía Motorizado.

Where are your favourite places to see live shows?

As I said, rock is on the margins, and that means sometimes places are not appropriate for either technical or infrastructure reasons. You get used to it but still you can't help but think that the bands deserve better. I think that Pura Vida for both musicians and the public is a great place.

Who are the local musical legends?

Obviously Los Redondos with their early *platense* formation lead the ranking of legendary status. But local rock music has many legends from incredible nights that have passed over the years. Many people compare La Plata to Manchester, it has mysticism and almost a band for every block.

If you had to pick an album of La Plata music to give to someone as a document of La Plata, what would it be?

For my tastes I recommend the first album of Los Peligrosos Gorriones, *Extraño Lugar de Estelares* and the red album from Norma.

How do you think that Argentine music is developing in general? What are the trends?

The Argentine mainstream hasn't taken any risks for close to a decade. Good albums are released but they've not reached the level of surprise or risk that I would like to hear. The risk is found in the underground, always. Bands like El Mato, Los Espíritus, Shaman, Un Planeta, they offer a more attractive movement. They work very professionally and offer first-rate shows without falling into demagoguery. Nor do I think there is a prevailing style, it seems to me that things have slowed a lot. Today at a show sometimes there are fans of various genres enjoying the music, whether an indie guitarist or someone else. It's creating tolerance and that's always good.

HERE, THERE AND EVERYWHERE

REMEMBERING 40 YEARS OF ARGENTINE ROCK

by Miguel David Grinberg

translated by Nicholas Nicou

In 1966, with Susana Salzamendi, the Argentine journalist and poet Miguel David Grinberg organised Aquí, Allá y en Todas Partes (the Spanish translation of The Beatles' "Here, There and Everywhere"). It was the first in a series of events that united talks from music journalists with rock concerts by some of the Argentine artists and bands then beginning to define what became rock nacional and would, in Grinberg's own words, become part of a generational movement. In 2007, to celebrate 40 years of Argentine rock, Ginsberg once again organised a Aquí, Allá y en Todas Partes event, a chance to look back at what had gone before and see how today's artists fit into the narrative.

Here are two essays written by Grinberg, one for the first event in 1966 and one for its anniversary 40 years later. In these texts we see the excitement of a generation wanting to be part of something bigger, followed by reflections on what actually transpired.

***

A city is like a person: it is born, it grows, and it becomes full of scars. A city dies when people abandon it; the same occurs with civilisations. Every one of us has left a piece of ourselves somewhere, in some building or other. A person's death is determined by a simple, dirty trick of physiology. We are more fragile than the city, but we have memory.

Those who have seen the sun rise in the sea, who have savoured the smell of gunpowder, or those who have ridden down a road on a motorcycle at top speed know that beyond the city (or perhaps closer to it), sometimes there is life. And just as one can die in such a way that nobody notices, there are ways of surviving which simulate death. None of that interests us. That is why we're dissatisfied.

We recall the itinerary of many young people from many cities. Young people who have walked the tightrope between these two ways of living. Some have found a way of growing up without conceding to the barbarity of everyday life. Watching those children's faces, those unbridled emotions, it is possible to make out the seeds of a new sensitivity: that of the troubadours, contemporaries emerging from that rubble named 'Social Life' and inheritors of a boundless lust for life. The secret lies in refusing to submit to the merchants of protest or the patrons of lies.

A person also ceases to exist when they lose their powers of invention, along with their ability to create things and experience excitement. And while the traditionalists and conformists grumble, the rest sing and enjoy all that can be enjoyed, in spite of the chaos and indifference.

Presentation for Aquí, Allá y en Todas Partes, Teatro de la Fábula, Buenos Aires, December 1966

INNOCENCE WILL NEVER SURRENDER

"One generation goes, another comes, but the land always remains..." Ecclesiastes

At root, it is about just one song, one which the young people sing with distinct melodies and seemingly different lyrics, here, there and everywhere. It unfurled during the second half of the 20th century while, in a number of places across the world, many young people were sent to kill or die in wars which, at root, were always the same, or who, alternatively, were hounded, repressed and rejected for the simple fact of being young and carrying that song in their hearts.

At a given moment, among us, like a light in the darkness of ritual genocides and filicides, a song emerged which broadcast the desire to live, dream and celebrate the gifts of existence without having to beg forgiveness for doing so. From whom exactly was one meant to beg forgiveness? From some 10,000 arrogant psychopaths who, in an alleged position of 'authority', manipulate the future of all humanity (over 6,500 million individuals today). Who gave them this criminal mandate? Was it a cannibalistic and troglodyte God who requires the constant sacrifice of whole generations through the doing of militaristic castes, abhorrent dictatorships, inhuman corporations and demented politicians? Was it a perverse virus which undermines the human capacity to love and share? Was it simply a dedication to barbarity which is recycled over time, creating new mechanisms of destruction and breeding fear and misery between peoples, who are transformed into herds or packs at the convenience of a monarch, a religious clique or a transnational company?

At once, in the midst of this oppressive situation, a troubadour appeared who sang: "There, far away, you can hear a love of spring which has gone wandering. Open the rain barrel, take a cup, and the glass man will vibrate again. You will speak with him on a direct line to infinity. And you will see that everything, everything is moving towards this moment – here, there, and everywhere". We owe this ballad, "Amor de Primavera" (Love of Spring), to Hernán Pujo and José Alberto Iglesias. For many young people on this earth, this resonated like a hymn.

In 1966, when rock was just starting to emerge in Argentina, the censors of the time labelled it protest music. Los Beatniks sang "Yeah, I'll be a rebel/ Yeah, a rebel 'til the end", and the electric guitars and the musicians' long hair led to the formation of a stereotype, in conventional society, of rockers as nonconformists. This was no exaggeration, as they did indeed reject the juvenile spirit of the time head-on, one which fulfilled a mould of 'formality and politeness' associated with happiness and the romanticism represented by pop music and its various televised figures, from the smile of Jolly Land and the "Pecos Bill" of Luis Aguilé, to the cover of "Only You" by Los Cinco Latinos or the "Canario Triste" of Elder Barber.

The troubadours were singing poets in the Middle Ages. The custom emerged in Provence (a former province of the southeast of France) ten centuries ago and the style flourished in the 12th century. Normally, the troubadours travelled over long distances, and they thus contributed to spreading news from region to region. With their love songs first and foremost – but also with their socialist propaganda compositions, their debates and, in short, their vision of the world – they established the principle of a cultural and political history with a variety which has not yet been found in any other document from the period.

Present studies on art and the troubadours highlight the fact that the protest song, with political content, has constituted a universal movement, especially in Latin American countries where singers of ballads and troubadours have played their part – usually accompanied by the guitar – in their capacity as singer-creators and author-interpreters. Subjects of social, protest or political content (although also prophetic), tend to constitute the main message of this 'troubadour' movement. In Cuba, this peaked in the 60s, giving rise to the movement called *nueva trova*. "A troubadour is a poet with a guitar", Silvio Rodríguz once said. Similarly, in Argentina we can speak of a 'trova rosarina'. Often, the 'political content' is surpassed by the 'poetic content' and the protest transforms into a celebration of harmony and fraternity. The Beatles, Bob Dylan, and our own Moris, Tanguito, Miguel Abuelo and León Gieco added undoubted flourishes to this tradition.

At the end of 1966, in Buenos Aires, some of us musicians and poets gathered together in a small theatre located in a basement in the neighbourhood of Abasto (traditionally associated with the legacy of Carlos Gardel, a troubadour in his own way) to pronounce our desire to grow and be part of a society in which plenitude was a human right. We did not propose inventing a new trend or founding a new movement; we felt part of a generational movement which, across the entire world, was saying 'no' to violence and 'yes' to the art of living and sharing. We felt a 'love of spring' which has gone wandering, and which, little by little, was being incarnated in a group of young people who chose parks as their stage: Plaza San Martín, Plaza Francia, Parque del Centenario. Hippies and artisans. Pacifism and ecology. Rockers and the rock public. Festivals and albums. Alternative magazines and experimental communities. The rest is history.

2007 came, and with it – as could be expected – came the celebration of '40 years' of Argentine rock. But behind the ritualistic conventions and an avalanche of books documenting unique chapters of this harmonic journey, a group of young people emerged who are once again tuning into a 'love of spring' which has gone wandering. There is always a generation reaching the art of existence. Its only script is imagination and tenderness. "There is not one being who lives life in vain; we all have a special mission, and it is up to every person to find their own and bring it to fruition in the best way possible". Last September 21st, a group of girls and boys were designing multicoloured T-shirts on the hill of Plaza San Martín bearing the phrase "I live in the universe", just a few steps away from the memorial honouring our fallen in the Guerra de Malvinas [Falklands War]. The land remains. The poem beats on. Innocence will never surrender.

Essay for 40th anniversary edition of Aquí, Allá y en Todas Partes in 2007

Inroducing Sebastian Litmanovich

You will have no doubt seen the illustrations by Sebastian Litmanovich that are dotted throughout this book. If that name doesn't seem familiar to you, it's perhaps because Sebastian is better known under his musical alias of Cineplexx. Making melodic pop music influenced by Velvet Underground, BMX Bandits, Flaming Lips and the Beach Boys, Cineplexx have released 11 full-length albums and have recorded with prominent indie-pop musicians like Duglas Stewart (BMX Bandits), Norman Blake (Teenage Fanclub) and Jad Fair over the years.

Yet, as well as being a musician, Sebastian is also a talented graphic designer and illustrator having set-up his own studio, Tea Time Studio, that he's been running since 2002, working with a mixture of corporate clients and artists, record labels and organisations from the music world.

The images that feature throughout this publication are from his *Illustration Series* of doodles, ideas and sketches.

Okey Banana by Sebastian Litmanovich

AUSTRAL AESTHETICS

GRUPO AUSTRAL AND THE SUCCESS OF THE BKF CHAIR

by Bennett Tucker

Between the late 1930s and the early 1940s, a new phase of modern development in architectural ideals and design aesthetics began to transform the urban fabric of Buenos Aires and its suburban surroundings. The vanguard of this new phase, the Grupo Austral, or Southern Group, would leave behind a lasting influence on future generations of Argentine architects and designers, and would have a wider influence on subsequent industrial design throughout the world. Although the group's activity as a movement within this wider phase was relatively short-lived (lasting from October 1939 until July 1941), they would nonetheless push Buenos Aires, and the country at large, forward into the twentieth-century as a strong modern cultural centre amidst the influx of progressive cities throughout Latin America.

The most lasting examples of the Austral aesthetic are found in two separate but closely connected iconic images: the group's Paraguay y Suipacha Atelier in downtown Buenos Aires, and more notably, the BKF Chair. Although the atelier is considered the embodiment of the Austral architectural ideals, it's the BKF chair that has gone down in history as the most acclaimed and widespread surviving image, one that is still immensely popular today yet continually overlooked and its origins often dissociated from those who designed it and the region from where it came. The BKF Chair, better known today as the Butterfly Chair, was a simple and organic design that resulted in immediate success, and has since remained as one of the world's most popular and desirable household items among both cultural elites and everyday consumers. The popularity of the chair and its association with the group's atelier and manifesto is a story that traverses continents and decades and is deeply embedded in the history of mid-twentieth century modernity.

By the turn of the twentieth century, the explosive export economy of Argentina had already established its capital city as one of the great cosmopolitan centres in Latin America, which resulted in a conservative urbanism so entrenched in Eurocentric academicism that no other comparison could be more fitting for this city than the 'Paris of South America'. By the late 1920s however, spurred on by the historic visit from the

Franco-Swiss modernist leader and visionary architect, Le Corbusier, the architectural aesthetic and urban fabric began to shift throughout Buenos Aires away from this academicism. Emerging modern architects and designers began to instil a fresh new idiom and vertical thrust into Buenos Aires, populating the city with high-rise structures and larger-scaled buildings by the mid 1930s.

It was against this background of modern urban transition that the two young architects and friends, Jorge Ferrari Hardoy and Juan Kurchan, graduated from the Facultad de Arquitectura at the University of Buenos Aires, and left their home country to pursue their self-education immersed in the capitals of Europe. During these travels, the architect duo soon found themselves in Paris knocking on the door of the prestigious Rue de Sevres 35 atelier of Le Corbusier. This proved to be perfect timing as Le Corbusier was then obsessed, following his first visit to Argentina, with the idea of redesigning the centre of Buenos Aires. Although his plan had yet to receive a commission from the Buenos Aires municipality, he nonetheless felt the two young Argentine architects could contribute advantageously through their many local contacts, and would hopefully persuade their own countrymen to eventually commission the plan. Therefore, in October 1937, the two young and ambitious men found themselves busy at work in the master's atelier.

Antonio Bonet (left) with Josep Lluís Sert and Le Corbusier (right)

When Hardoy and Kurchan returned home to Buenos Aires at the end of 1938, Alejandro Lapunzina, in his essay "From the Pampas to the Altiplano: The Master Plans of Le Corbusier in America," describes them as being filled with excitement by the experience of having worked with Le Corbusier and the echo that this produced. Their time away had reinforced their ambition to crystallize the new phase of modern urban transformation that was emerging in Buenos Aires under a new name: Grupo Austral, and under the guidance of their own manifesto. While in Paris, the two men had met the Catalan architect, Antonio Bonet, and reconnected with him back in Buenos Aires. Bonet, almost ten years their elder, and with a preestablished architectural identity, nonetheless accompanied the Argentine architects, establishing himself as the Grupo Austral's third founding member.

The creation of the group was the praxis of what Hardoy and Kurchan first developed while in Europe, but reserved for an exclusive Argentine language amidst the declining flow of modernism leaving Europe, the rise in popularity of North American industrial design, and the neighbouring modern enclaves developing in Latin America at the time. Today the Austral aesthetic is recognized by many art historians as the embodiment of the most influential and important stages in Argentine architecture and design. As Jorge Francisco Liernur and Pablo Pschepiurca describe in their book, La Red Austral, the group was paradigmatic with other regional currents, "self-conscious of its peripheral location," and oriented towards creating a new emerging cultural and technical centre.

The Grupo Austral also coincided with global and local events that would create impetus to their manifesto and would subsequently have a major impact on the design and success of the Suipacha Atelier and the BKF Chair. In La Red Austral, Liernur summarizes three of these events as: a continental period of discovery of Latin American architecture and theorizing about a new regionalism among emerging architects; the rise of 'organicism' in the US in the late 1930s leading to the popularity of organic furniture; and the arrival of surrealist exiles to New York City at the outset of hostilities in Europe. Likewise, in the exhibition catalogue "Latin America in Construction for the Museum of Modern Art", Silvio Plotquin considers the formation of the Grupo Austral as one of two major establishments in Buenos Aires that confronted the lingering old conservative academicism and paved the way to a future modern Argentine capital. The first was the creation of the Avenida 9 de Julio, the major north-south traffic artery running through the heart of downtown that "made radically clear the need for new models and ideas." The second was the creation of the Grupo Austral as a "collective conversation about the production and roles of architecture," noted Plotquin, "which proposed a formal, materials-oriented paradigm."

The Austral manifesto, published in 1939 in the periodical Our Architecture, would solidify the group's social and aesthetic convictions, providing the foundation for the designs of the Suipacha Atelier and the BKF Chair. "The [current] architecture has remained detached while urbanism has failed to solve the basic problems of modern cities," the three founders proclaimed in their manifesto, concluding that, "in Argentina these have not yet been raised." The manifesto also served as a severing point from the previous academicism, stating that these schools are "divorced of all architectural reality, and have contributed to the existing state of disorientation among the architects." The manifesto was also guided by Bonet's adherence to the surrealist establishment in Paris and its new foothold in New York City. The surrealist influence on the group was solidified as a relationship between architecture and painting. "The example that painting gives other visual arts," the manifesto states, "is by freeing themselves from any moral prejudice, social and aesthetic..." and it was precisely this "complete freedom that has allowed painting to reach surrealism." "Surrealism makes us reach the background of individual life," they concluded.

As noted before, the Suipacha Atelier was the archetypal example of the ideals expressed in the group's manifesto, and still stands today at the corner of Avenue Paraguay and Avenue Suipacha in downtown Buenos Aires. It was designed by Bonet, along with architects Vera Barros and Lopez Chas, and served as the place where the architect lived and worked alongside Hardoy and Kurchan. According to Federico Ortiz in his book *The Work of Antonio Bonet*, this construction was the first fully identifiable Argentine building within the mature contemporary movement and made clear the designer's intention, which served to document their new ideas. Everything from the materials used, the systematization of equipment, the use of colour and even the garden terraces legitimized the ideals expressed in the group's manifesto and brought refreshing change to the urban environment. "The work is extremely interesting," Ortiz notes, "while the structural clarity of the building is one of the remarkable aspects, it is from the spatial point of view that it acquires greater significance."

Atelier on the corner of Suipacha and Paraguay, Buenos Aires

The initial purpose of the BKF Chair, designed in 1938, was to fill the interior of the Suipacha Atelier, which it did after the first prototypes were produced in 1939. Although the future success of this iconic design was largely attributed to its new visual aesthetic, the original inspiration for the chair was taken from an earlier design in the mid 19th-century, known as the Tripolina Chair. The first appearances of this Tripolina design appeared in Italy around the 1850s as a field campaign chair during the Italian wars for unification. It consisted of a wooden folding frame that a canvas sling could be stretched over once the frame was standing, a convenient design for the mobile life of soldiers on campaign. By 1877 the British engineer, Joseph Beverly Fenby patented this design and the Italian military continued to make use of it during their colonial campaigns in North Africa, eventually adapting the name 'Tripolina'. The visual similarities between the Tripolina and the original BKF Chair design are easily identifiable. However, the three Austral designers, whose names create the chair's title (Bonet, Kurchan, Ferrari Hardoy) took this Italian model and by infusing it with their regional language, applying the surrealist influences of their manifesto, and conforming it to the minimalist and organic aesthetic emerging at the time, created an enduring and highly desired masterpiece.

The original BKF design does not fold like the Tripolina, but its frame consists of two tubular steel rods smoothly bent and welded together to create the rigid structure. Stretched over this frame are four reinforced pieces of leather sewn together and 'slung' – the chair is also known as the Sling Chair – over the corners of the frame to create the seat. This simple composition of integrating two contrasting and separate parts, the frame and the seat, is viewed by Liernur as a productive synthesis of elements from different worlds: industry and crafts, a synthesis that can been seen as a constant throughout Austral architecture as well. Both the Suipacha Atelier and Hardoy's Virrey del Pino apartment house in the Belgrano neighbourhood of Buenos Aires also combined contradictory but workable elements between industry and local artisanal culture.

It is through the chair's biomorphic shape that a connection exists between Bonet's rhetoric of surrealism and the design of the Suipacha Atelier. According to Liernur, Bonet believed that the application of "sinuous curves" was a more organic and creative expression over the straight-line aesthetic of the earlier European functionalism as seen in the Bauhaus and de Stijl influences. This curve was seen in the corner facade of the Suipacha Atelier as its upper stories extended out over the sidewalk in a sweeping glass curtain curve, and as the roof terraces curved in bulbous waves. On the rooftop, Ortiz observes "clear evidence of a gradual shift away from the rigidity of rationalism of the first period, which is confirmed by the use of curved shapes and ruled surfaces." Equally expressive, the presence of curves replaced any existence of rigid corners in the design of the BKF Chair. Every angle was smoothly rounded and bent into shape, while the straight lines of the frame were covered by the leather seat whose biomorphic shape was also one continuous flowing sinuous curve. "Such resonances [of sinuous curves]," notes Liernur, "are linked to the idea of expanding the degree of creative freedom, unlocking the unconsciousness of the way, they assumed, had succeeded in the surrealism painting potential."

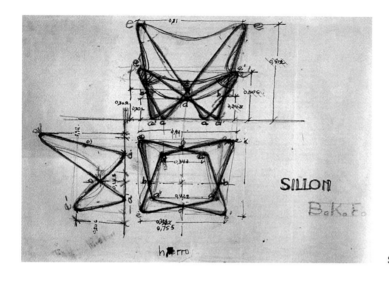

Sketch of BKF Chair

Likewise, the sturdy leather sling seat established a distinct local and regional dialect in design. References to the pampas and the Argentine hinterlands have often been associated with this use of rich fine leather. The outlining shape of the seat somewhat resembles that of a hide floor rug, and the craftsmanship of the external stitches on thick leather hints to a subtle Argentine rustic-chic appeal, a trending fashion today among mid-century furniture and interior design enthusiasts. The aesthetic look and simplicity also embodied a similar spirit to the furniture concurrently produced in North America, than to the academicism and functional Corbusian influence from across the Atlantic. The biomorphic shape of the frame and the womb-like outline and slope of the seat would soon establish a standard in the emerging category of 'organic furniture'.

This new, simple, organic look gave the chair immediate recognition. In 1940 it was debuted to the public at the design exhibition for the 3rd Salon de Artistas Decoradores in Buenos Aires, where it received notable prizes. In submitting the chair to the exhibition, the group attributed the design largely to the credit of Ferrari Hardoy, thus establishing the chair's popular alias as simply: the Hardoy Chair. Edgar Kaufmann Jr., curator at the Museum of Modern Art in New York City at the time, immediately acknowledged the chair's success at the Salon exhibition. Kaufmann ordered three pre-production chairs (for around $25 each) from the Austral atelier in response to its Buenos Aires debut and his own personal approval, finding the chair to be functional, handsome, lightweight and inexpensive.

As the BKF Chair entered the international stage, other magazines and exhibitions on both sides of the Atlantic immediately began promoting this new iconic product. In France, the director of the magazine Architecture d'Aujourd'hui began selectively manufacturing it for his subscribers under the name 'AA Chair'. In the US the manufacturer Artek, owned by the Finnish designer Alvar Aalto, produced the chair between 1941 and 1948 in large numbers to a readily accepting public, sending royalties back to Argentina. However, it was not until 1947, after a temporary decline in demand due to the war effort, that the manufacture Knoll Associates acquired the production rights and began producing it under a new lasting alias: the Butterfly Chair. With the growing international popularity of the Butterfly Chair design, manufacturers both big and small began to flood the market with a variety of unauthorized imitations, offering the chair at a low cost and in a variety of materials and colours.

By the end of the 1940s Knoll filed a lawsuit against competing companies producing similar designs, and as a result of a seminal court hearing in 1951, Knoll halted its manufacturing of the Butterfly Chair. The court ruling stated that Knoll could no longer sue other manufacturers for producing unauthorized reproductions of their Butterfly Chair design, and ultimately decided that Bonet, Kurchan and Hardoy's original design itself was too familiar to previous examples of the same design (notably the Tripolina Chair) for anyone to claim copyright protection. As the wooden mallet came slamming down at the final court ruling the legal floodgates were opened for anyone and everyone to produce this iconic chair. In the 1950s alone, Knoll estimated that no less than five million BKF-designed chairs were produced.

Today this court ruling still maintains the status quo. The market has, in its own way, established the boundaries between the $30 BKF style chair at Wal-Mart, popular with West Coast beach parties and for taking naps in college dorm rooms, and the $3,000 vintage designs from the Knoll era and contemporary high-end manufacturers, targeting modern furniture collectors, trendy city apartments, and rustic-chic country homes. The last resemblance to an authorized production could have been in the 1960s by the Argentine manufacturer, Six, only loosely considered legitimately 'authorized' because Juan Kurchan himself was a partner, almost two decades after the Grupo Austral had dissolved.

Looking back through the chair's widespread history it is evident that the influences and initiatives from the North American promoters – notably Kaufmann, Artek and Knoll – led the BKF Chair down the path to unfathomable international success, but also, because of this worldwide success, led to a blurring of identity and origin. Since the court's ruling after the Knoll lawsuit, the BKF Chair largely assumed international status in the minds of its consumers and collectors, a product belonging solely to the twentieth century rather than to a particular nationality.

In recent years, however, as mid-century modern furniture and design has seen a massive resurgence in popularity and in mainstream trends, the BKF Chair has reassumed its rightful place in the canon of desirable furniture design among such elites as Eames, Saarinen, Nelson and Bertoia. It is also through this popular resurgence that Argentina has reclaimed its chair as a national icon, thus progressively revealing to the international design community of artists and collectors the serious artistic

history and true national origins of the BKF Chair. In Buenos Aires today notable manufacturers such as BigBKF and serious design sellers such as Calma Chica are but two of the many *porteño* establishments promoting and supporting their national claim.

Probably no other piece of modern furniture or design can boast the widespread and international history as the BKF Chair. Designed by three architects who developed their skill and matured their ideas in the streets of 1930s Paris under one of the great modern visionaries of the 20th century; produced in the Austral spirit of surrealism infused with a regional dialect during Buenos Aires' most transitional period of urban design and architecture; and finally promoted and recognized worldwide through the initiatives of New York design enthusiasts under the new wave of organic household furniture. Although the history runs deep, the chair has nonetheless returned full circle from its international popularity, to find itself regarded today throughout Argentina and Buenos Aires as their national artistic contribution to mid-century modern design.

Adverts and record
covers highlighting
the popularity of
the BKF Chair

ANTI-UTOPIAS

UNDERSTANDING THE HAUNTING IMAGINATION OF IOSI HAVILIO

by Lorna Scott Fox

It's a testing time for writers. A mediatized, globalized, marketized culture, reinforced by social media, works to discourage originality and temper the pungency of the periphery. But a country with such a forceful literary tradition as Argentina's is better placed than most to produce arresting new voices. Its realism was always surreally unhinged, as in Roberto Arlt; its metaphysics always warmed by the material, as in Borges, or the ludic-fantastic, as in Cortázar; its intellectual horizons have always been international.

The five novels by Iosi Havilio (Buenos Aires, 1974) recombine those traditions in striking fashion for what are essentially elaborations of a fictional climate, a mood, which takes precedence over character and plot. When paradoxically transmitted in the first person, the effect is startling and seductive. *Open Door* (2006) is narrated by a veterinarian who drifts to a village after the inexplicable disappearance of her female lover, shacks up with an elderly odd-job man, dreams, gets bored, and plummets through a drug-soaked affair with perverse schoolgirl Eloísa. In the absence of backstory or introspection (replaced by a perpetual erotic hum) the stress falls on details and moments, visions and sensations. "With my back to the street, I caught my reflection in a long and narrow mirror with traditional painted designs around the edge. People passed to and fro and I appeared and disappeared between them." What's so liberating about this ambience is its decoupling of the personal from the psychological, allowing us to inhabit a depthless, affectless consciousness spread lightly as a web over a mysterious reality at once mundane and extreme.

Extremity dominates Havilio's next novel, *Estocolmo* (2010), a plunge into the guilt and terror accompanying – again – passivity, as a gay Chilean exile returns home pursued by his psychotic Balkan lover. René's humiliations and rationalizations were perhaps overwrought, and Havilio returned to the narrator of *Open Door* for a glacial, glittering sequel, *Paradises* (2012). The death of her husband sends our vet to the sordid edge-lands of Buenos Aires, where she works in the reptile house; Eloísa is there too, in a variously disabled, marginal milieu updating the underworlds of Arlt and Manuel Puig. The narrator's trademark apathy, even toward her small son, at once smothers and heightens the alienation of a world where the poison of the paradise berries contains its own antidote – if anyone could remember how that worked.

At this point Havilio began, he has said, to feel 'domesticated' by his own manner.

Iosi Havilio,
Agencia Literaria CBQ

He promptly upset expectations with *La Serenidad* (2014), an anything-but-serene discharge of mischief and mayhem befalling The Protagonist and other functionally named figures, under Quixotesque chapter headings beginning "In Which ...", and embellished with pictures and diagrams. This protagonist equates more overtly to the author: one theme is harassment by the past, with a younger self firing paper aeroplanes at him that draw blood. Like a zestful preparatory notebook, *La Serenidad* piles on the ingredients that could feed into a work of fiction, dispensing with the conventions of fiction itself for a gleeful exercise in avant-garde expressionism.

While letting rip with this, Havilio was also composing the tightly condensed *Petite Fleur* (2015). Elements spilled across, notably the closeness of author and character – it's a more private tactic, but they happen to live in the same house in the same small town – and the haunting by a younger, more promising self. And since Havilio is always in dialogue with his work (which, like Roberto Bolaño's, could be called a single oeuvre under construction), he reprises older scenes, such as the media scrum viewed from afar, swarming round a bridge suicide, that triggered a fleeting breakdown in the narrator of *Open Door*.

Here the incident is the explosion of the fireworks factory where the narrator was employed. As a result José becomes reluctantly responsible for home and toddler, while wife Laura earns their keep. But his momentary catatonia before the fire shifted something deep inside. Soon José finds himself killing the next-door neighbour every Thursday, with ritual inventiveness, always to the strains of the eponymous jazz number. The brilliance of *Petite Fleur*, told in one headlong paragraph alternating comedy, horror, nostalgia and speculation, is to merge a chamber piece about gender roles and marital ennui with a wild metaphysical fantasy, united by the notion of routine. José wrestles earnestly with life in death and hate in love, gradually opting for the guidance of signs 'from the beyond'. At least he tried. As Havilio quipped in a 2014 interview: "It takes many bad philosophers forever going in circles to salvage the flower of thought."

Havilio's heroes are typically in the grip of some unfathomable crisis, which uncannily focuses their perceptions yet puts the world at a remove. Scraps of popular, mass and elite culture flicker in the background like the recurrent unattended TV, some surging briefly to the fore, often in distorted form (José's love for Tolstoy's *Resurrection* ignores its social outrage). The same goes for political and historical phenomena. Havilio has observed that he cannot claim to any romance of family militancy during the dark years. It's tempting to detect hints of social-political concern: when José obsessively watches the factory burn on the internet, "the crackling flashes reminiscent of a far-off,

IOSI HAVILIO
AFTERWORD BY OSCAR GUARDIOLA-RIVERA

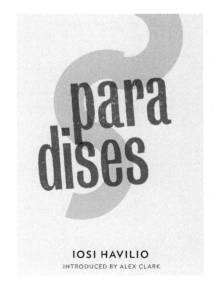

IOSI HAVILIO
INTRODUCED BY ALEX CLARK

spectacular war," is he deploring the west's mediatic air strikes? When in *Paradises*, the narrator survives on the edge among other damaged souls, is this about Argentina's turn-of-the-century debt crisis, describing the "aftermath of apocalypse", as one critic put it? Is René's condition as a Chilean exile more than a springboard for fear? No, or not primarily. Unlike an older writer such as Ricardo Piglia, Havilio is not codifying neo-liberalism. His very contemporary spirit treats the signs of the world, present or past, cultural or political, as a store of equivalences that touch his characters, wrapped in their quasi-autistic subjectivity, by virtue of whim or chance.

The overarching existential metaphor is that of the (real) madhouse in *Open Door*. In 1898 the asylum of that name was founded in Luján, following the enlightened 'Scottish system', in which inmates roam free inside a verdant compound. "No walls restrict the horizon, nothing to limit the illusion of absolute liberty," says a period document copied down by the narrator, whose village is attached to the asylum. The inmates enjoy good food, dances, games; "blacksmiths, carpenters, tailors and bakers work from morning to night, some single-mindedly, others dreaming ..." This harmonious utopia strictly for crazies is recalled by the ironic title of *La Serenidad*, and in *Petite Fleur* by the volunteers at a plant nursery parodying the Tolstoian communal ideal.

With their thrilling dynamic of ruptures and buried connections, Havilio's mood-fictions are ruled not by harmony but by instability, caprice and superstition. His drifters often yearn to be rooted, plant-like, in the earth; they're not quite mad enough to think that they are free.

THIRD CINEMA

TOWARDS A REVOLUTIONARY CINEMA

by Lina Samoili

"For the first time, we demonstrated that it was possible to produce and distribute a film in a non-liberated country with the specific aim of contributing to the political process of liberation." Octavio Getino

Produced in Argentina in 1968 by the directors Octavio Getino and Fernando Solanas, *La Hora de Los Hornos* (The Hour of the Furnaces) is a distinct example of revolutionary cinema. By using radical methods of production and distribution, its creators managed to attract a wide audience and bring political and social matters up for discussion. *La Hora de Los Hornos* is without doubt the most important cinematic expression of the values and aesthetics of Third Cinema.

Third Cinema was a radical and political cinematic movement that first appeared in the 1960s and 1970s in Latin America, before later spreading to Africa and Asia. This innovative film movement was greatly inspired by the Cuban Revolution of the 1950s and Brazil's Cinema Novo. Its name was invented by Solanas and Getino as a response to the predominant tendencies of what they identified as First and Second Cinema. First Cinema referenced the commercial scope of the Hollywood studios, and its penchant for big commercial movies structured around social stereotypes and bourgeois values. Second Cinema, meanwhile, presented an alternative to the American 'mass production' system through European art films, which, despite offering new aesthetic innovations and possibilities, lacked when expressing strong political viewpoints. Third Cinema was therefore conceived as a means of encapsulating revolutionary ideals corresponding to the sociopolitical circumstances of the period. It was a strong response to the established cinema of the 1960s.

"Third cinema is, in our opinion, the cinema that recognises [...] the great possibility of constructing a liberated personality with each person as the starting point – in a word, the decolonisation of culture." (Getino, Solanas, 1969)

The directors of this cinematic movement, that included fellow Argentine Raymond Glevzer, Chile's Patricio Guzmán and Bolivia's Jorge Sanjines, focused on highly political, topical and localised subject matter: identity and community, migration and exile, colonialism and emancipation of the oppressed. National liberation and independence were particularly frequent themes in their agenda. The emergence and evolution of Third Cinema was awarded further agency by the fact that the 1960s and 70s saw intense political conflict with the emergence of various guerrilla movements (e.g. FARC in Colombia, Tupamaros in Uruguay), coups d'état (e.g. Pinochet in Chile in 1973, Videla in Argentina in 1976) and US intervention across Latin America.

In the late-1960s Solanas and Getino wrote the essay-manifesto "Towards a Third Cinema", in which they laid out their radical interpretation towards contemporary cinema and its place within political discourse. They argued the need for revolutionary symbolism in film-making and they pointed out the role of militant cinema, especially during that particular historical period (after the Cuban revolution and the Vietnamese struggle). As mentioned in the essay: "A new historical situation and a new man born in the process of the anti-imperialist struggle demanded a new, revolutionary attitude from the film-makers of the world". They emphasized the responsibility of intellectuals and artists in anti-imperialist struggles such as those in Cuba and Vietnam.

GRAN PREMIO Y PREMIO FIPRESCI.
IV FESTIVAL INTERNACIONAL
DEL NUEVO CINE.
Pesaro. Italia. 1968

UN FILM DEL
GRUPO CINE LIBERACION

LA HORA DE LOS HORNOS

Realizado por:
Fernando "Pino" Solanas

Investigación y Guión:

According to their essay, revolutionary cinema directly attacks the system and cannot be assimilated by it. In their critique auteur cinema (European art house) was not an alternative to the Hollywood studios as it failed to produce a strong political critique towards the capitalist system and remained, as Solanas and Getino wrote: "'trapped inside the fortress' as [Jean-Luc] Godard put it". Documentary represented the main basis of revolutionary film-making, due to its ability to reflect social realities through imagery which cannot be digested by the system. Indeed, Third Cinema film-makers primarily made socio-political documentaries on the state of countries within Latin America. Nonetheless, the themes addressed in Solanas' few fiction films, such as *The South* (1998) and *Tangos, the Exile of Gardel* (1985), unravel in a social and political context. For example, *The South* is concerned with the story of Floreal, who after being released from prison after the end of the military dictatorship in Argentina in 1983, remembers the black days of the coup and his imprisonment; *Tangos, the Exile of Gardel* deals with a group of Argentinean artists exiled in Paris, who long for their homeland and culture.

La Hora de Los Hornos, described by Sight and Sound as "the paradigm of revolutionary activist cinema" is a four-and-a-half-hour documentary divided into three parts: "Neocolonialism and Violence", "Act for Liberation" and "Violence and Liberation". Through its exploration of the whole history of Argentina starting from its first years following independence, it offers an analytical, powerful and radical examination of the sociopolitical, economical and cultural development of Argentina. It brought to the forefront of discussion matters of neocolonialism and imperialism in Latin America, and especially Argentina.

Due to the dictatorship of Juan Carlos Onganía in the 1960s, the film was only privately screened in Argentina. As Nicole Brenez wrote: "To attend a screening was in itself a political act, transforming spectators into responsible historical subjects, not because they did or did not agree with the content of the film, but by virtue of the very decision to attend, despite the threat."

In the introduction to Part One, the directors pay homage to the Cuban Revolution ('the only liberated country') and Che Guevara. From the very beginning, the audience are fed quotations from significant revolutionary leaders and intellectuals, such as Fidel Castro, Che Guevara, Frantz Fanon and Hernández Arregui, giving a strong and clear sense of the film's radical content. Combined with the fast, rhythmic score the directors create an imposing cinematic effect attacking the audience's passivity and keeping them motivated and alert. From a Marxist perspective, the documentary describes in detail how the USA's intervention in Argentina's economy in the 1950s-60s helped create conditions that led to daily violence, poor living conditions, an income gap between social classes, political violence in the 50s, the fall of Perón, the ascendance of the dictatorships and the economic, political and cultural dependence on Spain, England and USA.

As with their essay "Towards a Third Cinema", Solanas' and Getino's documentary is also preoccupied with the responsibilities of artists and intellectuals – their responsibility to contribute to the preparation of the revolution through their artistic and scientific means. Part one, "Neocolonialism and Violence", reveals the integration of intellectuals into the system and the ideological war between the capitalist system and the subversive transmission of ideas though the media. The second part, "Act for Liberation" suggests the connection of the intellectuals with the middle class, and their non-involvement in the rise of the left and the revolution. Finally, part three, "Violence and Liberation" portrays how state violence and its mechanisms are used to fight any revolutionary action. The narration now takes a more active role, as it not only shows, explains and guides, but also proposes. It clearly encourages the audience and the nation of Argentina to 'create its own revolution', to create 'another Vietnam' and, as Che Guevara encouraged, "another Cuban Revolution".

The film's revolutionary character and innovative style had a major effect on significant directors and intellectuals. As Nicole Brenez explains: "Later visual essayists such as Chris Marker, the Dziga Vertov Group, the Cinéthique Group, Patricio Guzmán and Alexander Kluge were inspired by the film's elegant radicalism".

Another characteristic example of this militant cinema is the documentary *La Batalla de Chile* (The Battle of Chile). Directed by the Chilean director Patricio Guzmán, it offers a chronicle of his country's political struggle in 1973, depicting the upper class's attempts to depose the government of Salvador Allende, US intervention in Chile's domestic politics, the coup d'état against Allende and the establishment of the military dictatorship of Augusto Pinochet.

Guzmán was directing a separate film about the first 12 months of Allende's government, his first feature *El Primer Año* (The First Year), when he realized that something powerfully anti-democratic was taking place in his country and began work on *La Batalla de Chile*. In a similar direction to *La Hora de Los Hornos*, the film is divided into three separate parts ("The Insurrection of the Bourgeoisie", "The Coup d'état", "Popular Power"), each of them released 2 or 3 years apart. The combination of archive footage and narration takes the form of reportage. However, the messages and the indications towards the audience are so concrete and straightforward, that it reaches the zenith of what we can call socially-engaged art. The most striking scene is undoubtedly the shocking moment in which Argentine cameraman Leonardo Henrichsen films his own death during the failed coup attempt of 29th June.

La Hora de Los Hornos and *La Batalla de Chile* examine the social realities of their respective countries, while also offering suggestions and encouragement to advance the anti-imperialist struggle. As Solanas and Getino argue in their essay: "Revolutionary cinema is not fundamentally one which illustrates, documents, or passively establishes a situation: rather, it attempts to intervene in the situation as an element providing thrust or rectification. To put it another way, it provides discovery through transformation."

Despite Solanas and Getino's intentions and efforts, Third Cinema did not manage to expand sufficiently and gain mass appeal. Its values and aesthetics remained quite restricted and unfortunately it failed to have a significant contribution to the evolution of cinema. As Sara Saljoughi mentions in her essay "Third Cinema Now": "Film Studies has relegated Third Cinema to a mere example (of counter-cinema or political cinema)... In the current mode of Film Studies, Third Cinema is an "'old' thing that can barely keep up with the thirst for the new."

However, this cinematic movement had a certain influence in Europe and especially Britain. Although Latin America, Africa and Asia were the nucleus and basis where Third Cinema emerged and developed, we cannot deny the fact that elements of this radical cinematic expression can be found in other film tendencies too. The Black Audio Film Collective, formed in the UK in the 1980s, produced a number of experimental films which were "a new variation of Third Cinema", according to Marzano in his article "The Art of Hunger: Redefining Third Cinema". Adapted for the British socio-political circumstances of the 1980s, the Black Audio Film Collective used Third Cinema's tools and guidelines to make documentaries that addressed themes of race, diaspora, memory and political struggle, such as *Handsworth Songs* (2012) and *Testament* (1988).

Without a doubt, Third Cinema took a unique approach to film-making and offered an alternative voice to the western cinema of the 1960s. It encapsulated social injustice, working class struggle and the repression of the state and the bourgeoisie to promote the idea of revolution as the clearest path to a better future and more equal society.

MOTHERS OF THE STRUGGLE

THE MOTHERS OF PLAZA DE MAYO ARE STILL STANDING STRONG DESPITE THEIR ADVANCING YEARS

by Nick MacWilliam

"First they ignore you, then they laugh at you, then they fight you, then you win."
- Mahatma Gandhi

For the Mothers of Plaza de Mayo (Madres de Plaza de Mayo), 11 August 2016 was a momentous occasion. The date marked the 2,000th consecutive Thursday that the internationally-renowned human rights organisation has congregated in the Buenos Aires central square from which they take their name – location of the presidential Casa Rosada (Pink House) – to demand the return of their children disappeared during Argentina's military dictatorship of 1976-83.

The women were accompanied by supporters and other citizens who had lost loved ones to state terrorism perpetrated against students, activists, union members and anyone else considered a 'subversive' by the authorities. Most of the 30,000 victims were young, most of them innocent of any crime, yet the state and its backers within Argentina and abroad co-opted the language of counter-terrorism to eradicate the growing political consciousness and organisational capacity of a new generation of Argentineans who believed that a fairer society was both a right and an obligation.

Under the governments of husband-and-wife Néstor Kirchner (2003-07) and Cristina Fernández (2007-15), the Mothers worked closely with the Argentinean state in convicting those involved in human rights abuses under military rule, with the country today boasting an unparalleled record of transitional justice in Latin America. Much of this is down to the campaigning of human rights organisations such as Las Madres, who maintained their fight despite the dictatorship amnesty granted by former president Carlos Menem following his election in 1989.

However, the mutual support which characterised the Mothers' relationship to the *kirchnerista* governments ended with Fernández standing down at the 2015 presidential election. Her successor, the neo-liberal conservative Mauricio Macri, has brought struggle back to the forefront of the Mothers' mandate. And their response to Macri's regressive policies has proven that, though they get older and their numbers fewer, the fire of resistance burns as fiercely as ever.

THE MILITARY JUNTA

Argentina's military junta came to power on 16 March 1976 in a coup d'état against the government of Isabel Perón, who had taken over the presidency two years earlier following the death of her husband Juan Perón. Following the coup, the military began systematically eliminating anyone suspected of leftist sympathies, with the primary targets being students and other young people whose political development had been conditioned in relation to their compatriot Che Guevara and the Paris '68 uprising. The military sought to uphold the conservative pillars of church and private capital, both of which ran contrary to the socialist principles of many Argentines who populated universities and factories.

With the backing of the US government, Argentina adopted many of the methods of General Pinochet's regime in neighbouring Chile, kidnapping and torturing opponents before killing them and disposing of the bodies so that they would never be found. The strategy of disappearing people had a dual function: it promoted the shock doctrine climate of terror necessary to quell resistance to neo-liberal reforms while distancing the state from responsibility for the killings.

These were the conditions under which a group of middle-aged women began assembling in the Plaza de Mayo to demand information about their missing children. Having been ignored in their individual pleas to the authorities, which had of course orchestrated the disappearances, the women found strength in unity. They had initially turned to standard avenues in their hunt for information: they went to the police, the Ministry of the Interior, the church. While these undertakings failed to turn up any leads, they brought the women into contact with one another; solidarity would form a defining element of their struggle.

On 30 April 1977, a Saturday, 13 mothers of disappeared children congregated in the Plaza de Mayo. They were led by Azucena Villaflor, whose son Néstor and his wife Raquel Mangin had been abducted. Downtown Buenos Aires was not as busy as during office hours, and so the decision was taken to switch to Thursdays in order to make the protests more visible. The day has stuck ever since.

As Argentina's repression intensified, an increasing number of women were demanding answers as to the whereabouts of their sons and daughters. The movement now known as Las Madres de Plaza de Mayo was growing in size and stature, as the women's presence and resolution drew attention to the brutality of Argentina's military dictatorship. The white headscarves they wore represented human rights and maternity and would become recognised around the world as symbols of the Mothers' struggle.

The authorities ignored the women at first, hoping they would soon grow tired. When that tactic failed, the state terror apparatus was applied. On 10 December 1977, the Mothers of Plaza de Mayo took out a newspaper advertisement to publicise the names of their disappeared children. That same night, the organisation's leader Azucena Villaflor and two other members, Esther Careaga and María Eugenia Bianco, were abducted from their homes. They were taken to the naval academy in Buenos Aires, which had been converted into a detention and torture centre by the military. They were not seen again until their remains were identified in 2005.

Argentina's return to democracy in 1983 failed to dampen the Mothers' resolve. After all, it was not democracy they were demanding, but the return of their children. The civilian government of Raúl Alfonsín staged trials of military figures, which determined the guilt of the ruling generals such as Jorge Rafael Videla, Emilio Massera and Leopoldo Galtieri. In 1985, however, President Alfonsín introduced amnesty laws which prevented further trials. His successor Carlos Menem then pardoned the generals and released them from prison.

BUILDING THE POST DICTATORSHIP

The 2003 election of Néstor Kirchner shifted the political landscape of Argentina's new democratic era. One of his first acts was to order the removal of portraits of the generals from the military academy where they had hung since the dictatorship. This symbolic act set the tone for the convictions of over 1,000 people connected to the abuses of military rule. General Videla and General Reynaldo Bignone were among those given multiple life sentences. Videla, whose five-year rule oversaw the most intense repression, died in prison in 2013. Bignone was sentenced in 2010 for kidnapping and murder, in one of multiple trials which found him guilty of atrocities. Among the abuses committed by the men was the separation of hundreds of babies from their biological mothers, who were subsequently executed. The babies were given to regime-friendly families.

The presidencies of Néstor Kirchner and Cristina Fernández supported the human rights campaigns being waged by the Mothers and the similar-yet-unconnected Grandmothers of Plaza de Mayo, who dedicate themselves to reuniting the stolen children with their biological families, with around 120 people identified to date. The Mothers worked closely with the government in pursuing human rights abusers and developing a support network for dictatorship victims and marginalized social groups. Despite the presence of allies in the Casa Rosada, however, the Mothers were largely unable to determine what had happened to their loved ones.

40 years have passed since the implementation of state terror in Argentina and the Mothers are today fewer in number, as their numbers inevitably decrease through the passage of time. The cruelty of military rule is reflected in the endless cycle of Thursdays: these women swore to be there every week until their children were returned. Now, in the winter of their lives, the likelihood is they will never know.

THE EMPIRE STRIKES BACK

While nobody could fault the elderly women for withdrawing from the public eye, recent events in Argentina have galvanised the social justice and human rights movements. The election of Mauricio Macri in December 2015 brought Argentina firmly back under the neo-liberal banner of the Washington Consensus, which the Kirchners had rejected in favour of a regionalist alignment with other left-wing governments in Latin America. The Mothers have played a major role in opposing this new status quo.

So far, Macri has introduced huge hikes in utility bills, the removal of export tariffs for agricultural exports (leaving Argentinean citizens effectively subsidising the wealthy landowning lobby) and the removal of currency controls which sent the cost of living soaring. Tens of thousands of public sector workers have been fired since Macri's election, while independent media has been curtailed in an effort to suppress dissenting voices. Macri has also sought to criminalize acts of social protest, most notably in the controversial jailing of Milagro Sala, leader of the Tupac Amaru organisation, which receives state subsidies to construct social housing in Jujuy, northern Argentina. While these policies have engendered large-scale organised resistance among diverse sectors of Argentine society, they have endeared the president to Washington DC and Wall Street. This is particularly true with regards the US vulture fund speculators who have made billions out of Argentina's economic misery during the early 21st century by buying up debt at a fraction of its worth and then hitting the country for the full amount.

Most worryingly for organisations such as the Mothers of Plaza de Mayo, Macri's election signalled a drastic ideological shift to the right. Argentina has turned its back on the progressive regionalism that under the Kirchners underpinned its relations with other left wing governments in Latin America in favour of close alliance with the United States. Following Macri's agreement to pay billions of dollars to the 'vultures', Barack Obama scheduled a visit to Argentina, the only member of the G20 bloc of nations he had not yet visited during his presidency. With impeccable timing, Obama's trip coincided exactly with the 40th anniversary of the military coup. Many saw a correlation between the vulture settlement and the official visit of the US president to the country at such a poignant moment. The decision caused much anger in Argentina. Especially as in 2016 the US state department declassified documents showing Washington had supported and even encouraged the military junta in its assassination programme against leftists.

According to these documents, the then-Secretary of State Henry Kissinger was in close contact with the regime generals. "Our basic attitude is that we would like you to succeed," he is reported to have told them. "I have an old-fashioned view that friends ought to be supported. What is not understood in the United States is that you have a civil war. We read about human rights problems, but not the context."

Following public outrage, it was announced Obama would spend 16 March, the anniversary, in the southern resort city of Bariloche rather than in Buenos Aires, where large demonstrations were scheduled. The furore confirmed the suspicions of the Mothers and many others of Macri's affiliation to the military regime.

Shortly before the presidential inauguration on 10 December 2015, the Mothers' long-serving president Hebe de Bonafini announced a protest in Plaza de Mayo for that day. The Macri family business profited handsomely during military rule, as the forced implementation of neo-liberal policies reversed worker rights and flooded the domestic market with cheap foreign imports.

The right wing media, meanwhile, was emboldened by the new politics of Macri. The day after the election, La Nación published an editorial calling for the release of dictatorship officials and comparing the human rights movement, symbolised in Argentina by the Mothers, to fascism. Dictatorship victims were compared with the perpetrators of recent terror attacks in Paris that killed over 100 people. Whether he wanted to or not, Macri's election had brought the legacy of military rule, and its ongoing conflict of ideologies, into the mainstream.

The era of forced disappearances may have ended, but other anti-democratic practices serve to maintain the neo-liberal hegemony in place. The government has targeted the Mothers in the same way as they did with Tupac Amaru's jailed leader Milagro Sala. In August 2016, a Buenos Aires judge ordered the arrest of Hebe de Bonafini after she refused to submit to questioning over the embezzlement of funds designated for a housing project coordinated by the Mothers. In response, hundreds of supporters confronted police and prevented them from reaching any of the Mothers, while former ministers of the Fernández government were among those to attend a rally later that day in the Plaza de Mayo in solidarity with the Mothers.

Since Macri's assumption of the presidency, arms sales from the US have increased in what some perceive as the first step in extracting the vast untapped mineral resources which lie beneath Argentinean soil. In other parts of Latin America, militarization has been a notable aspect of the extraction process, as communities which oppose the pollution of their environments face state repression designed to benefit the foreign companies working there. Further, increased military cooperation opens the door to the potential construction of a US military base in southern Patagonia which will provide access to huge freshwater reserves that will become increasingly important throughout the 21st century and beyond.

For those opposed to the reinforcement of the neo-liberal model in Argentina, these are times of concern. The Mothers of Plaza de Mayo can offer guidance. Argentineans will require similar levels of dedication and courageousness if they are to construct the fair and humane society originally envisaged by the country's murdered generation of activists and subsequently taken up by their mothers, who channelled their grief into a cohesive and influential structure of popular resistance and transitional justice. The lessons of the past are clear: the path of the future less so.

ART OF PARTICIPATION

PRINT WORKSHOPS OF PROTEST

by Ellen Gordon

Tumultuous times breed works of art that express the confusion, offence and fear in the air whilst demonstrations and acts of protest mark discontent and call outside attention to a problem. Whether loud, peaceful or violent, they are always charged with emotion. The purpose of protest is to express a feeling or idea and to make it known to a wider audience, and this is where art and protest find common ground. The world of art is often criticised for being exclusive, for catering only to a select few and for creating an elitist language of expression that alienates the wider population. However, as in the work of the Taller Popular de Serigrafía (The Popular Silk Printing Workshop), when the participation of the general public is essential to the creation of an artwork, we see that these criticisms cannot be applied to art as a whole. An outlet can be found for any kind of expression, and when creation allows real participation there are no exclusive boundaries.

The Taller Popular de Serigrafía was established in 2002 as an artistic movement working with The Popular Assembly of San Telmo, one of Buenos Aires' oldest neighbourhood. The Assembly was born in the wake of civil revolt following the protests and unrest of 2001, which saw then-President Fernando de la Rúa accused of inertia over corruption amongst the government offices. The country had been in a state of economic crisis for three years and the public rose up against the government with a series of protests, even withdrawing their money from banks in November 2001 to such an extent that they brought the entire Argentine banking system to the point of collapse.

This public outrage intensified and came to a head in December 2001. The imposition of restrictions on cash withdrawals caused huge problems and delays for the population,

Memoria Colectiva, May 2002
Anniversary of the Trelew Massacre

worsening the already tense economic state of the country, and further diminishing faith in the government. Protesters began looting and outbreaks of violence were reported all over the country. A state of emergency was declared on 19 December, but the violence and *cacerolazos* (protesters banging pots and pans) continued. By the following day, 26 people had died in violent clashes around the country. President de la Rúa resigned and famously escaped in a helicopter from the top of La Casa Rosada, the government palace in Buenos Aires. The country was to have five different presidents within the next two weeks.

The Taller Popular began working with the San Telmo Assembly in February 2002 to create an art of participation within the context of social justice and protest movements. The group began to put this into practise by holding open serigraphy (silk printing) classes and creating slogans with locals for a day of reflection to commemorate the violent military coup of March 1976, collectively remembering another complex and violent chapter in the country's past. In April 2002, the group of artists printed banners in Plaza Dorrego, a main square in San Telmo with the phrase "otro primero de mayo en lucha" (another first of May at war), to remind the public of the protests and unrest of the previous year, and of many other protests in recent Argentine history. Bringing people together to reflect on their shared recent history is key to the Taller Popular's work. By creating the images and phrases with locals, instead of imposing slogans devised solely by artists, these banners were artworks of participation.

Local factory workers, upon seeing the images in Plaza Dorrego, invited the Taller Popular de Serigrafía to join them in a protest on 1 May to demand worker-led nation-alisation of the factories owned by the companies they worked for. Slogans were created during the demonstration and printed by the Taller Popular de Serigrafía alongside the protesters. The group went on to join in many protests with workers and other city residents, printing images to commemorate previous protests and to accompany new ones. They became particularly notorious in connection with the workers of the textile company Brukman who took over the Buenos Aires factory, abandoned by the company's owners in the crisis of 2001, and began to run the production line on their own. The workers decided upon fair wages for themselves, gained new clients and received support from many social organisations and artists. The Brukman owners and the police tried time and time again to evict the workers using threats and violence, and the Taller Popular de Serigrafía rallied support in the workers protests by printing phrases such as "Cultura Obrera" (Workers' Culture) and "Fábricas recuperadas en pie" (Recuperated factories still standing). The workers and the Taller Popular carried out a 'Maquinazo', making all kinds of items of clothing printed with phrases and images associated with the protest. With the aim of showing solidarity to other evicted workers in similar situations around the city and reclaiming workers' rights to their work, the Brukman workers and the artists created a camp made out of metres of fabric. This sparked a week of cultural activity with other artistic groups in the square where the camp was made.

The Taller Popular also joined those denouncing the deaths caused by the unrest as

Maquinazo, 7/05/03
Print on ready-made garments made by the workers of '18 de Diciembre' cooperative, which would then be donated to flood victims in Santa Fe province

Brukman es de las Trabajores, April 2003
In support of the workers of the '18 de Diciembre' cooperative, at that point evicted from their factory

well as government and police repression. In June 2002 protesters Darío Santillán and Maximiliano Kosteki were murdered near Avellanada station in Buenos Aires whilst picketing at an event known as the massacre of Avellanada. The two young men, members of different workers' rights groups, were joined by many other picketers making their way to the centre of Buenos Aires. The federal, national and city police violently impeded the protesters' way into the city and as a result of the clash Santillán and Kosteki were shot. During demonstrations to denounce violence and the deaths of these men, the Taller Popular printed images of Santillán and Kosteki, accompanied by phrases such as "hablamos por los que fueron callados" ("we speak for those who were silenced").

Through these forms of expression, the Taller Popular joined together acts of protest and the creation of artworks. The key element is participation, as without the protesters the art loses meaning; and without the artists there is no printing. The line between artist and protester is blurred, as the two come together as co-creators, relying on the emotion and spirit of a moment to create a print and capturing the collective need to protest. The workshop is brought to the street and the group provides a medium for expression without imposing a particular style, as the technique and aesthetics of the works are products of a specific situation. Improvisation, constant redefinition and adaptation lie at the heart of the movement, and these qualities place the power of the movement into both the worker's and protesters' hands, as well as the artists'.

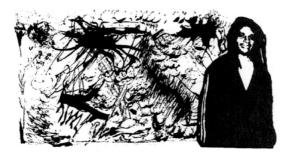

Maxi Kosteki, 19/10/02
Homage to Maximiliano Kosteki, DarIo Santillan and Carlos Almiron in
Lanús station, the neighbourhood where they lived, worked and studied

Dario y Maxi – Trabajo, Dignidad, Cambio Social, 26/07/02
Printed during a cultural meeting in Puente Pueyrredon one month
after the assassinations of Maximiliano Kosteki and Daro Santillan

This sense of equality in the Taller Popular de Serigrafía's work generates a collective memory with each piece of clothing or fabric printed. Whilst each individual piece will have individual memories attached to it, the repetition of phrases and images creates a wider connection to all those who took part in the protest. No rules or particular stylistic features are required to produce this kind of work, the phrases can be simple or more complex and are sometimes printed alone or with images, place names and dates, but the printer and the fabric provide an essential tangible base. The fact that an open and indignant expression of emotion is required to produce these physical objects makes the printer akin to a translator creating a concrete version of an otherwise ephemeral emotion.

Whilst memory serves those who took part, the pieces are bound to moments in the past and can be used as props to tell a story. Even if versions of the complex stories differ, these props give the storytellers a physical marker from which to hang their stories. They can also be used to draw global attention to the problems faced by the Argentine public. They have been used precisely in this way at various gallery exhibitions and also at the São Paulo Biennale, as the Taller Popular de Serigrafía's work has gained international recognition. The prints show the universal capacity to protest in a display of discontent that most people will see reflected in aspects of their own society, whilst maintaining the sense of contextual meaning; a specific, Argentinean story of resilience.

It is surely impossible to have a book about Argentina without someone drinking mate, so here it is (photo by Adam Fry)

DISPLACING RATIONALITY

THE ROCK AND PROTEST POSTER SANTI POZZI

by Russell Slater

interview translated by Nicholas Nicou

Santi Pozzi is a graphic designer responsible for some of the finest rock posters you'll see anywhere in the world. Whether creating posters for local bands like El de Prietto Viaja Al Cosmos Con Mariano and Los Alamos or international acts like Pearl Jam and Tame Impala, you can be sure that Santi's designs will be bold, full of texture and with a revolutionary spirit that fits perfectly with the rock bands he often works with.

On the following pages though we wanted to show you the diverse work he's created, from protest posters to folk images as well as the obligatory gig poster.

***

When did you first become interested in design?

When I was young, I really liked comic books and illustrated books; I spent a lot

of time looking at the images. In my room, I had a Snoopy poster which was an offset lithograph from the 70s that I loved. But I think that the thing that had the biggest impact was seeing an exhibition on psychedelic rock posters in San Francisco. That was the moment when I said to myself: "this is what I want to do".

Who was your greatest inspiration as an artist?

I'm not sure. I guess that there's a lot of Victor Moscoso in my work; he's a poster designer whose work I love. I also really like the Argentine pop wave of design from the 60s, such as the work of Edgardo Giménez and other designers like De Lorenzi, Fontana, Gonzalez Ruíz and Distefano.

Many of your designs are centred on rock. What's your relationship with it?

I like all kinds of music, but when I was a teenager I listened to nothing but 60s rock, and it was the cover art for those records which drew me to design.

I think that the contemporary rock which is on offer is very rich in variety and quality. A great deal of really good and really distinct bands are playing on the same stages, and it's really inspiring to work with the artists that you listen to. I prefer to listen to independent musicians rather than mainstream music because those guys are like me: they have a life like mine and talk about things which

also happen to me.

How can the national obsession with rock music in Argentina be explained?

I'm not sure if there's an 'obsession'; I think that there's a very rich tradition of rock bands, which has served as an outlet in different eras in a society which is so repressed.

In some of your posters, you can see the influence of indigenous cultures in the colours and symbols you use. What is your interest there?

I am drawn by psychedelia because it plays with casting doubt on the very act of

visual or auditory perception, highlighting how arbitrary it is and overwhelming the senses in order to displace rational attention. I think that psychedelia offers you a more transcendental type of connection, and, in that way, it's tied to pre-Hispanic cultures and their spiritual relationship with nature, free of the Judeo-Christian paradigm or the cult of Greco-Roman reason.

You did a series of posters about the educational system in Argentina, which were against CoNEAU [the Argentine National Commission of University Assessment and Accreditation] and in favour of public education. Can you tell us a bit about the story behind these images? What causes were you supporting?

On different occasions, I gave public classes on silk-screen printing and produced free public posters. I think that this is just another way of communicating a message and one which is especially participatory in nature, where people can learn, take part, and print their own posters, which they then take out with them on a march or put up at home. The message is adopted and transmitted in all of these situations.

During the last protest, we were specifically demanding a larger budget for public universities, in order to tackle the exorbitant price hikes being imposed by the new government, as well as continuing to demand higher salaries for the teaching staff, many of whom are paid a low wage or forced to work for free.

ARGENTINE HIP HOP

EVOLUTION OF A SCENE

by Juan Data

The idea of a hip-hop scene thriving in Argentina may sound paradoxical to foreigners. Not only because we are talking about the most predominantly white and Eurocentric country in Latin America but also, and mainly, because of Argentina's long history as the main purveyor of *rock en español* on the continent.

Argentina is essentially a rocker country where the so-called *rock nacional* dominates both the mainstream airwaves and the underground scene of pretty much every big city. Hip-hop then was born as a movement of resistance, by urban kids from the fringes of Argentine pop culture that couldn't find a place for themselves in the local rock-dominated music spectrum. Thus hip-hop in Argentina is essentially a subculture of opposition. During most of its development, hip-hop has struggled to detach itself from the ubiquitous rock scene and claim an identity of its own.

It may not have the same sociological implications of racial segregation as other more multiracial countries, like neighbouring Brazil, where hip-hop became intimately associated with the experience of Afro-descendents of the low-income outskirts of the big cities. But adopters of hip-hop culture and rap music artists in Argentina always felt marginal and disenfranchised, surrounded by an hegemonic and hostile rock-centric environment that mocked them and didn't take them seriously.

'That's music for blacks and there's no significant black population here, so rap will never work in this market,' was a mantra we heard all the time in those days, anathema to many Argentine b-boys of the early days, who were day-dreaming of building a hip-hop scene in Buenos Aires. Record labels, show promoters, music journalists, concert venues, they all dismissed hip-hop, considering it a childish passing fad that would never amount to anything in a country so proud of its European aesthetics and British-influenced rock.

It's curious, but other cultural expressions of explicit Afro roots, like reggae or the blues, were easily embraced by that same establishment. Hip-hop, however, was deemed too foreign – and too American. Both reggae and the blues were accepted by Argentines probably because they came with the seal of approval of British tastemakers. Argentina's pop culture compass has always been more aligned with the old rather than the new empire.

B-BOY STANCE, THE FIRST GENERATION

Like almost every other country outside of the United States, we got our first taste of hip-hop culture through the breakdance movies of the early 80s. Those highly influential low-budget flicks turned teenagers into b-boys overnight across the globe, and Argentine youngsters were no exception. Once the fad passed, however, only a few remained loyal and kept exploring what was behind that urban subculture. Ridiculed by the rocker establishment, the first generation Argentine b-boys were forced to retreat and regroup in the darkest, most remote corners of the underground.

A select group of these kids survived the late 80s dark age, settling in the working-class suburb of Morón. Today they are widely regarded as the founding fathers of the scene. Amongst them, three young aspiring MCs started spitting rhymes in Spanish without any role models available, simply emulating the flow of the American rappers of the time, and trying to make it fit to the particular phonetics of Argentine Spanish. Their stage names were Mike Dee, Jazzy Mel and Frost.

Mike Dee was the most visible of that bunch, mainly for being a rare Afro-Argentine, which helped him get hired by mainstream TV shows to perform pantomime-like interpretations of his art form. He also had a short cameo in an album by the popular ska band Los Fabulosos Cadillacs.

Jazzy Mel was, however, the one who got the first recording deal in the early 90s. After releasing two albums in São Paulo, Brazil, the Uruguayan-born MC returned to Buenos Aires and signed a contract with a dance-oriented label. Inspired by the European wave of hip-house of the day, the label was looking for a local rapper who could do pop, radio-friendly, club-oriented, rap hits aimed at middle class teenagers. Frustrated after being turned down by all other labels, Jazzy Mel saw no better chance to show his talent and signed.

Between 1991 and 1992 Jazzy Mel enjoyed superstardom in Argentina's mainstream. He helped incorporate the word rap into the local vernacular, and while his music was cheesy and his rhymes were rather basic, he inspired a whole second generation of kids to adopt hip-hop as their tribal identity (hiding in plain view, next to the Euro-dance-sounding smash hits, Jazzy Mel's repertoire included less popular tracks where he explained hip-hop culture in surprising depth and dropped names of true-school genre architects, laying the ground for his young fan base to do more research).

During the boom of Jazzy Mel's mainstream overexposure Argentina's rock scene went into an odd phase when everybody and their mothers embarrassed themselves recording wacky rap songs without any prior knowledge of the culture. Respected rock legends like Charly García, Fito Páez, León Gieco and many more experimented with rap during this period, further ruining the reputation of the genre and unleashing a disco sucks-like backlash. Also, a handful of clones of Jazzy Mel tried to get a piece of the pie and unanimously failed horribly.

Left: Unknown b-boy headspinning at La Negra nightclub, circa 1999 (photo by Juan Data)

Below: Unknown b-boys dancing at a jam in the west-side outskirts of Buenos Aires, circa 2000 (photo by Juan Data)

Mike Dee on stage at Cemento, with Mr Funky standing behind him, during a Bola 8 show, circa 1997 (photo by Gabriel Di Matteo)

Mike Dee and DJ Magic Boy behind the decks at a hip-hop concert in Cemento circa 1997 (photo by Gabriel Di Matteo)

The exception to the rule, the anomaly in this story, has to be the case of Illya Kuryaki & The Valderramas. They were the age of Jazzy Mel fans at the moment of their debut, 14 and 15 years old, and initially moulded their sound and aesthetics after The Beastie Boys of *Licensed To Ill*. They got signed by a major label exclusively because one of the two teenagers was the son of Argentine rock demigod Luis Alberto Spinetta. In a sense, the rock connection gave them the attention of the rock establishment and they took advantage of it. Over two decades later (albeit completely detached from their Beastie origins and rebranded as Rick James-like funk stars) they still enjoy mainstream success even if they never got fully accepted by the orthodox hip-hop fans who accuse them of being rich boys with no street cred.

BIRTH OF A SCENE

While neighbour countries like Brazil, Chile and even Uruguay were already releasing serious hip-hop albums, Argentina's hip-hop scene had to wait until 1997 for its long-delayed official debut. About a year earlier, an indie rock manager saw the chance of making a buck with this untapped market and wrangled together all the up-and-coming hip-hop artists that were unable to make noise on their own in the Buenos Aires' underground. He packaged them as a collective and presented them to the audience and the media as the latest novelty to hit the country's shores. Soon after that, I started publishing the first hip-hop fanzine, which for a couple of crucial years remained the only media that covered hip-hop in Argentina. The fanzine also helped connect Buenos Aires' underground with the scattered hip-hop heads in the rest of the country, thus the national scene started to take shape.

The debut album, the foundational piece of Argentina's current hip-hop scene, was a sub-par compilation titled *Nación Hip-Hop*, released with major label support and with the seal of approval of respected rocker Zeta Bosio (of Soda Stereo) as overseeing producer (because you still needed some rocker cred to get any media attention in Argentina at that point). The compilation featured a 'who's who' of the hip-hop scene of its day, along with plenty of participation by the 80s generation: Mike Dee recorded two tracks as Bola 8, Frost, even though he didn't record, was by the time of the release part of Sindicato Argentino del Hip-Hop, the flagship group of the collective, and Jazzy Mel participated behind the scenes, as recording engineer and producer.

Long gone were the embarrassing euro-dance hits of the early 90s, now the scene was mainly influenced by two dominant trends: the stoner East LA Chicano rap of Cypress Hill and the g-funk of 2Pac and Dr. Dre. Nobody in the collective was aiming for a specific sound, song topics or even aesthetics that truly represented Argentina, it was almost all derivative of Californian rap of the day. The only exception to that could be found in Sindicato Argentino del Hip-Hop who timidly started sampling tangos around those days and evoking the myth of the *pampas payador* (a South American troubadour from the 19th century, deeply connected to gaucho culture) as the ancestral roots of Argentine rap. Unfortunately none of that was ever included in their official recordings.

The compilation was a commercial failure, followed by other even sadder attempts by the same manager and his collective. Then, by the end of the millennia, a trio of MCs named La Organización emerged on the scene and changed the game forever.

La Organización brought with them a new way of rapping, mainly influenced by New York's gritty underground, but also by French and Spanish rap. Their battle rhymes were plagued with witty references to local culture and, more importantly, their pronunciation and slang were Argentine to the core. While most previous Argentine MCs used the informal 'tu' for the singular second person, La Organización stood out by emphasizing the use of 'vos', as is common in the colloquial parlance of their area. That might sound like a minor detail to foreign ears, but it was a big deal at the time.

Even though La Organización revolutionized the underground, they never left behind any proper recording that justified their legendary status. Before releasing their debut they broke up and only a handful of unfinished bootlegged demos survived them. However, the ripples of La Organización's revolution can still be felt today. One of the three MCs in that group, the freestyle champion Mustafá Yoda, launched a successful solo career soon after the break-up and within a few years became a sort of local rap mogul, launching the careers of many younger artists that have ruled the scene until today, starting a label (Sudametrica) and producing his own series of national freestyle competitions.

FLIRTING WITH THE MAINSTREAM

After they broke off from their manager, Sindicato Argentino Del Hip-Hop, attempted to go mainstream in 2001, when they signed with a major label. Their official debut album felt like a compromise between their street-savvy style and the expectations of the famous pop-rock producer the label assigned to supervise the recording. The first single was, in fact, built over a sample of "Mil Horas" by Los Abuelos De La Nada, an Argentine pop-rock anthem of the early 80s. That song granted them commercial radio airplay and even prime-time TV exposure, something unheard of for hip-hop artists in Argentina. And that wasn't all; that same year they were awarded a Latin Grammy in the urban category!

Unfortunately for them, their days as scene rulers were soon over. In 2003 a beef broke out between Sindicato and Koxmoz and the latter single-handedly destroyed the former's career once and for all with a hit song ("Al Toke") that's one of the all-time classics of the genre in Argentina. Koxmoz, by the way, are no other than the remaining two members of La Organización, joined by production visionary Kox-T and a newcomer MC.

Along with Mustafá Yoda and his protégés (Iluminados, Sandoval, Armamentales), Koxmoz ruled the scene for the rest of the decade. While Koxmoz were taking their rap into uncharted territories with risky experimentation, futuristic beats and brutally honest lyrics, Mustafá Yoda embodied the archetype of the modern Argentine rapper, honing his poetry with the spirits of urban tango and the *payador* culture while sticking

Frost, with Smoler behind him, two of the
four MCs of Sindicato Argentino del Hip-
Hop, circa 1998 (photo by Gabriel Di Matteo)

Above: Sindicato Argentino Del Hip Hop full lineup circa 1998, during the shooting of their first video clip for the song "Del Barrio", the first Argentine hip-hop single to go on rotation in Latin American MTV

Mustafa Yoda and Apolo during one of the rare live presentations of La Organización (minus Chili Parker) at La Meka, circa 2000

to orthodox boom-bap beats for his production. Koxmoz had their 15 minutes of global exposure with "Mi Confesión", a track they recorded as guests of French electro-tango pioneers Gotan Project, and their 2007 album didn't disappoint but also didn't gather the attention they expected either, maybe because of being too far ahead of their time. Meanwhile Mustafá Yoda toured every province of Argentina, neighbour countries and Spain, spreading his gospel and inspiring kids everywhere to follow his teachings. His second album, *Imaquinar*, in collaboration with Chilean producer Manuvers, also came out in 2007 and became the ultimate masterpiece of Argentine hip-hop. The genre had finally reached maturity and both the public and the critics were able to appreciate this without the need for any gimmicky fusions or alliances with the decaying rock establishment.

Another strong contender for the throne during that decade was Mustafá Yoda's nemesis: Frescolate. A former breakdancing champion, Frescolate garnered global attention in 2002 when he became the first winner of an international freestyle battle that included representatives of all the Spanish-speaking world. Diametrically opposed to the dead-serious approach of Mustafá and his acolytes, Frescolate fills his rhymes with a sense of humour and mainstream pop references, making it more accessible to the masses. He's also known for craving the attention of the cameras and when he's not a guest at a talk show or recording a commercial, he's freestyling from his bedroom to his thousands of YouTube channel subscribers.

NEXT LEVEL

By the beginning of the second decade of the century, hip-hop in Argentina wasn't an obscure, underground genre fighting for a place amongst the rock ubiquity any more. Argentine hip-hop is now its own established scene, with its own styles and codes and representatives in virtually every city across the country. It's still vastly dismissed by the mainstream music industry and gets zero play on commercial radios, but the country as a whole is aware of its existence: in 2014 Mustafá Yoda opened a public appearance by the then-president with a freestyle and it was simultaneously broadcast on every TV station. It could not be denied anymore, hip-hop was here to stay.

The new generation of MCs that compete for control of the scene were born after the Jazzy Mel boom and came of age in the globalization era, so they don't feel it necessary to go knocking on the doors of major record labels or begging rockers for their approval. The internet provided them with channels to distribute their music democratically and anyway rock, while still massive, lost some of its power with the rise of other popular genres like cumbia and EDM. More importantly, the current generation of MCs grew up listening to rap in their own language, without phony accents or foreign slang, and built their style based on that. Amongst the most remarkable of these there's Emanero, Frane & La Conección Real, Vasuras Crew, Juanito Flow, Marciano's Crew and many others.

During her first visit to Buenos Aires in 2000, Chilean rapper Ana Tijoux (back then still known as Anita, from the group Makiza) did a live freestyle on Plur FM with members of La Organización. (photo by Juan Data)

Derek of Sindicato Argentino del Hip-Hop during a show at Roxy, circa 1996 (photo by Gabriel Di Matteo)

BUENOS AIRES RAP
by JACOB LASSAR

Buenos Aires Rap is a documentary about the hip-hop scene in Buenos Aires today. But it's more than that. Directors Diane Ghogomu, Segundo Bercetche and Sebastian Muñoz have taken hip-hop and used it as a framework to portray a snapshot of the variations of life in contemporary Buenos Aires. It's a stunning piece of film-making, with characters as dynamic and engaging as the music they're making, as well as beautiful shots of the city, from the streets of the provincial slums to the clubs in the city centre. Here is a segment of an interview I made with co-director Diane, where we talked about the movie, hip-hop in Buenos Aires, and Afro-Argentineans.

Can you explain the importance of hip-hop in contemporary Afro-Argentine identity?

Afro-Argentine identity is something which is going through a very interesting moment, in that it is pretty much the first time in about 200 years that this community is being recognised as a part of the wider Argentine people. For example, in the census that took place in 2010 'Afro-Argentinean' was recognised as a possible ethnicity for the first time in these 200 years. Why the gap, you're wondering? Because Afro-Argentineans had essentially been written out of the nation's history following the wars of independence. They didn't fit in with the European, white ideals of the nation-builders and so their presence was essentially ignored. In recent years we've had global anti-racism movements which have forced Argentina to change and to recognise this Afro-Argentine presence in their history and their contemporary identity.

One of the consequences of this historical gap is that today's Afro-Argentine community, especially young people, don't really have a reference point in terms of their cultural place in this nation. That's where hip-hop comes in. When hip-hop was blowing up in the US in the 80s, and in Spain in the 90s, images of stars such as Public Enemy made their way over here, and the Afro-Argentine community was like, 'oh! There I am!' They began to see themselves represented as cultural and historical contributors, in a way which was not compatible with Argentine historical discourse.

So what's the scene like here in Buenos Aires?

I think one of the most interesting things for me, as a North American, has been seeing the range in styles and how these different styles come from different aspects of US or Spanish hip-hop that have been appropriated from the videos they see on YouTube or wherever. So you've got the people who are grabbing from the old school, looking at people like Public Enemy and the breakdancing crew Wildstyle, and they are like 'ah, ok, so this is hip-hop.' They're seeing something which was born from dilapidated communities in the US, a product of Reaganism, where people are speaking out about their realities. So it's that conscious hip-hop, people talking about politics in their raps, people who are more into the words than the production. But then you've got the younger generation, who are into their Lil Wayne and their Drake and for them hip-hop is about fun! It's just good music that people have fun to.

WALLS WITH STORIES

STREET ART IN ARGENTINA

by Ana Young

Buenos Aires is regarded as one of the must-see cities for graffiti and street art, cited by Huffington Post and Conde Nast Traveller as one of the world's capitals for this particular discipline. Starting off as a means of expressing one's feelings towards the political climate in the country, street art in Argentina soon found itself at the vanguard of a worldwide movement during the late 90s and early 00s, when the style could be seen as being at its zenith. These days, the informality of the streets has been replaced by organised exhibitions, commissions and the involvement of art galleries in creating a new image and preconceived idea of artists. The streets of Buenos Aires are still packed with art, beautifying the city's many abandoned buildings and bare walls, and bringing splashes of colour into an otherwise bare South American metropolis. But, how did it all start?

THE VOICE OF THE STREET

Street art in Argentina started through the medium of stencils as a way of protesting against the military junta that was in power between 1976 and 1983; once democracy had returned, people took to the street to express what had been repressed for all of those years. The most significant event, and the catalyst, for the use of stencils in Argentina was an event on 21st September 1983 that became known as 'El Siluetazo'. Working alongside the Mothers and Grandmothers of the Plaza de Mayo, as well as other human rights organisations and political activists, and in protest at the 30,000 disappearances that happened during the military regime, three visual artists (Rodolfo Aguerreberry, Julio Flores and Guillermo Kexel) conceived of the idea. For *El Siluetazo* they created an improvised workshop in the Plaza de Mayo where they asked the public to lie down and be traced, with these body outlines then being turned into

El Siluetazo (photo by Eduardo Gil)

One of Fernando Traverso's bicycles in Rosario

silhouettes that were pasted onto walls and monuments across the city. Each stencil could represent the memory of someone that had disappeared during the regime. It set a tone for the use of stencils, and particularly life-size silhouettes, that would continue for many years in Argentina.

A similarly-powerful project can be found in Rosario, where 350 bicycle stencils were emblazoned on walls and trees throughout the city in 2001 by Fernando Traverso, in honour of the 350 inhabitants of Rosario who 'went missing' during the dictatorship. The popularity of stencil work endured during the economic crisis of 2001, and following both the police shootings of student protesters Darío Santillán and Maximiliano Kosteki in 2002 and República Cromañón nightclub fire of 2004, all of which provided impetus for new works.

Writing or stencilling on walls became a way to force the public into paying attention to alternative versions of what was happening in the country, questioning whether these official means of news-telling were trustworthy; grand words and complex sentences were omitted, replaced by simple language that made the message accessible. Stencils were used in a repetitive fashion that created a relentless, unavoidable message across the city, something that its residents became used to and even welcomed.

ARGENTINA'S PLACE IN THE WORLD

In the 90s a new movement of street art blossomed, moving away from the use of stencils and political messages, to a more aesthetically pleasing style. In this regard, Buenos Aires was recognised alongside other major cities as a hub for a new worldwide street art movement. It was at the beginning of this period that the DOMA collective and StudioCHU established their name in Buenos Aires, at the same time that Banksy began focusing on his stencil work in England and the Brazilian brothers OSGEMEOS became an internationally known name after the exposure they were given in the New York-based 12oz Prophet Magazine. From the 90s to the mid-00s Argentine street artists helped break the taboo image of graffiti as vandalism, instead allowing it to be seen as a recognised art form. During this period spontaneity and the way in which

Mural by Poeta

the art was realised was essential, as well as the need to create artworks that could be more visually accessible to those who may have otherwise turned a blind eye to it. Street art began to be seen as 'art'.

A major factor in the proliferation of street art in Buenos Aires was that there weren't, and still aren't, restrictions on where artists are allowed to paint, nor do they need to apply for special permits in order to produce their art. It created the perfect environment for Buenos Aires' street art scene to develop, allowing artists to take their time and giving them enough psychological freedom to develop their own style. Artists could spend more time planning, and subsequently producing bigger and better murals uninterrupted, and without fear of persecution. The city itself began to ask artists to take part in projects to regenerate areas of Buenos Aires that found themselves abandoned.

STREET ART MOVES INTO THE MAINSTREAM

In 2009, the Argentine Director General's Office in Buenos Aires stated that, be it political or artistic, street art is good and welcomed, it is part of the city and it does not bother its public. By the end of the 00s it is fair to say that street art had moved away from its origins, becoming more recognised and official in nature, even approved by the government. Street art moved from the political to the professional. Argentina was not alone in this shift. Renowned street art researcher Rafael Schacter sees the boom period for street art worldwide as being between 1998 and 2008, an idea agreed with by Julian Manzelli, a member of the DOMA Collective. "The graffiti movement not only established itself in Buenos Aires, it also expanded along different tangents. Contemporary neomuralism, post-graffiti, graffiturism, decorative muralism, intermuralism, public art, adbusting, conceptual urban art, and many others! What you mostly see in Buenos Aires at the moment is decorative art with very little social and

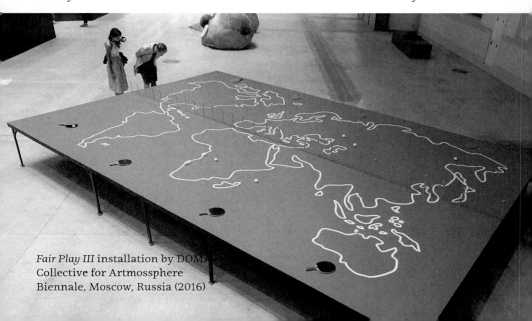

Fair Play III installation by DOMA Collective for Artmossphere Biennale, Moscow, Russia (2016)

political messages; it is completely different to how the essence of the movement was at the start."

These days many organisations and institutions are involved in street art projects across the city. The non-profit Graffitimundo has facilitated mural and art commissions for individuals, social organisations, local businesses and multinational brands such as Google and Facebook. Graffitimundo also run a gallery, Galeria UNION, that works to make profits for both the gallery and its artists, such as Cabaio, Jaz and Christian Riffel aka Poeta.

Google Cultural Institute now has a virtual library that catalogues and documents Buenos Aires' street art thanks to a partnership made in 2014 with the Buenos Aires Street Art association. Artists working on murals in the city have the freedom to choose their subject, including politically influenced pieces (though those tend to be rare these days). Artists have made clear that their aim is to propagate happiness through their work, using the brightest of colours and drawing from personal experiences.

The city's new generation of artists – Ice, Itu and Lean Frezzera for example – have carried the same tradition as their 90s counterparts and maintained relationships with international artists and collaborations. The first Meeting of Styles festival in Buenos Aires in 2011 saw many Latin American artists working together, including Peruvians Entes and Pésimo, Chilean AISLAP and Paraguayan Oz.

Christian Riffel aka Poeta once mainly worked on the streets of Buenos Aires and was highly involved in the growing graffiti scene of the 90s. Christian spoke to us about the importance of the transition from the street to galleries, and showed us that an artist does not have to restrict themselves to only one artistic outlet: "Nowadays my work is mainly created in my studio. I'm working on moving and static sculptures, adding light to the works and analysing their shadows; I'm using low-capacity motors and LED lights to produce movement. I'm also working on starting an art workshop with Leila Tschopp. I'm painting more on canvases than murals, in an attempt to enter the contemporary art scene of Buenos Aires, that is in fact very small and carries a stigma with urban artists, a stigma I'd like to eradicate. I have set up my own solo exhibition *A Ver Solo Se Aprende Mirando* at Galeria UNION. I will never stop painting on the streets even though I'm focusing on this now, because it is something I love to do. Painting in Buenos Aires is a beautiful experience; I love the connection it creates amongst people. It would be great to create a sculpture to be placed on one of Buenos Aires' streets."

We asked Christian what he thought of the statement that Buenos Aires is one of the street art capitals of the world. "I suppose it is true", he replied. "One of the benefits of painting here is the ability to paint the city itself. More often than not, people give permission to paint their walls and others are very kind and thankful for the paintings once they are done [without their initial consent]. This all helps the art grow." When we asked Julian Manzelli the same question, we got a slightly different view of it; "[Buenos Aires] is a city in which the movement has become very prominent in the last few years and has played a major part in the art movement globally. But New York, Barcelona, Berlin and São Paulo are the capitals, and they beat us in reputation by far!"

How about the views of art historians, like Rafael Schacter who believes street art, at its apogee, died in 2008 with the gallery exhibition in the Centro Cultural Recoleta? Both Julian and Christian seem to doubt the statement. "From what I understand, many artists from then on took on what was their hobby, as a legitimate profession," says Christian. "Many became very successful in that environment," he continues. "It gave them the confidence to paint in the streets in front of people. For me the scene and its community of artists hasn't stopped growing to this day." Julian also pinpoints that "the historically called 'original street art' by academics is a term that most of the artists involved in the movement never accepted or felt comfortable, and always avoiding using it." Supporting Christian's point about the growth of the scene, he says that the financial backing by organisations has been very important for artists; "In my career, I've had the benefit of having private businesses or individuals that became interested in my work and within their capabilities, have helped me out. I value and respect anyone who decides to get involved in the scene by helping artists out, it creates a beautiful connection between us. Without help, I would never have grown into the artist I am today."

SEE FOR YOURSELF

Tourists, photographers, fans and street artists from all over the world travel to Buenos Aires to experience entire neighbourhoods whose walls have been transformed by street artists, revelling in the colours of gigantic and intricate murals. Tours – which can be arranged by Graffitimundo and Buenos Aires' Arts Organisation – will allow you to see for example, works by Omar Gasparini ("Bienvenidos a La Boca") found on Av Almirante Brown 36; Villa Urquiza is one of the most famous areas of Buenos Aires for tour groups to visit and one can see why. The once completely abandoned area has been revitalised and now carries works by Martin Ron, Lean Frizzera, and even Italian artist Blu who made his mark by creating three murals in the area, as well as using the area for the creation of his award-winning stop-motion film between the years of 2007 and 2008 (*MUTO, Wall-painted Animation*). Underground stations have also become the location for large murals since 2013, and in 2014 a group of nine artists got involved in turning the walls of two underground platforms into a mural showing the beauty of the jungle and its native inhabitants at Federico Lacroze's underground station.

In 2012 Graffitimundo and Buenos Aires Arts Organization joined forces with White Wall Industries to produce a successful documentary about Buenos Aires' tough past. This film, *White Walls Say Nothing: Buenos Aires Street Art & Activism*, is a good introduction to Buenos Aires' street art past and how "the walls of Buenos Aires became the voice of its people", according to the film's makers.

If you travel around Argentina you will see tributes to Gauchito Gil along many of the main roads, especially in the north-eastern and central provinces. Gil is the most popular gaucho saint in Argentina due to his Robin Hood-esque reputation for helping those in need.

He is pictured above (left) with San La Muerte (right) (photo by Sergio Serrano)

A SERIOUS RESPONSIBILITY

THE SERENE STREET PORTRAITS OF POL CORONA

by Ellen Gordon

After a childhood in France and Madrid, Pol Corona only moved to Buenos Aires, his mother's birthplace, in 2004. It is a city that he has since adopted, and where his distinctive street art can be seen dotted across the walls, especially in the southern Barracas neighbourhood that he calls home.

The faces, shapes and natural forms that Corona paints are calming, striking and beautiful, and it is with a sense of calm, understanding and dedication that the artist explained to me the responsibility that he now feels as a street artist in the city.

When did you begin to make street art?

I started when I was 13 years old, just painting graffiti in the street. I'm French and I was born in Perpignan in the South of France. So my Dad is French and my Mum is Argentinean. When I was really small, maybe two years old, I moved to Madrid. I grew up there and lived there for 14 years, so at some point I started painting graffiti there. Graffiti was really what got me started, and claiming the right to paint in the streets.

My brother painted too, and we used to go out with a friend to paint graffiti in the streets. I really liked it and I met some people my age who were doing the same thing so we started going out to paint together. At this time, we were basically making illegal

graffiti and vandalizing by painting on trains and on the streets.

So did things change when you moved to Argentina?

In 2004 I moved to Argentina, and when I moved I carried on painting graffiti. At one point in 2007, due partly to the people I was getting to know and partly to the way the city is, in that it's very different from Madrid – it's a different world with a different history – I started seeing the streets in a different way and I started moving further and further away from graffiti. I felt different. The sense of vandalism and illegality became lost in a city that is so much more open, friendly, and ready to welcome colours and murals.

In Europe the reception to graffiti and street art is completely different?

Graffiti arrived in Europe about 15 to 20 years before it arrived in Argentina. Perhaps in Brazil, Chile and even Colombia graffiti was there but in Argentina it took some time to arrive. What I'm saying is that the word graffiti in Europe had already been categorised as something bad and aggressive that belongs to gangs, and is associated with illegality, destruction and vandalism.

Of course nowadays it might be changing. People in Europe are starting to relate more to urban art. Now there are many people involved in street art, who paint or make urban art, and so it's becoming more accepted. It's moving away from the perception of vandalism, and many people who make graffiti today are recognized as artists.

Did your work change in terms of style as a result of the move away from Europe?

My work changed completely. I am not a trained artist, I never studied anything. I never learnt to paint with anyone in particular. I just learned alongside my friends. When I was here in 2007 I started to draw a bit more, and to do other kinds of pieces in the street. That is how I started to grow and develop my painting a bit more. Today I feel that I do painting rather than anything else.

Your style is quite different from some street art. It seems human in that the forms are relatable and can be recognised. It doesn't come across as code. Is this something that you do consciously?

A style takes shape with the time dedicated to creating pieces. Time spent in the studio, time spent practicing helps to define a style. Mine is much more open than graffiti which tends to be letters and fonts painted for and to communicate with the graffiti audience. Murals and painting in the street is more figurative. The image is much more readable for any kind of person who happens to be on the street. Painting a face reaches much further than painting letters. People can see it more clearly.

So in this way your art becomes something for everyone, and not a form of rebellion

or protest?

Exactly it becomes a much more open language than graffiti, with a much wider audience, without that being the main intention. Having a wider audience was never my intention. My intention was always to paint in the street, as simple as that.

However you do realise that by painting in the street, whether you like it or not, you are imposing an image on public life and on the people who are in the street. This means that you have to take responsibility for what you paint. For example I would never paint weapons in the street. It is a subject that I would never touch upon. I would never paint a gun in the street, no matter what message it would bring.

So as a street artist do you feel that you have a responsibility towards the city and its people?

Yes, but I think that everyone who is on the street. whether they are painting, walking, working or doing whatever they might be, has a social responsibility. They are in a public space. So the responsibility for me is in the production of the image that I am imposing, and this is a serious responsibility. Coming back to the example of weapons, it represents many delicate issues for humanity: violence, borders and differences, etc.

I generally paint faces, and these faces tend to have a serene expression. They are not particularly emotional. This is how I feel that I am, and I try to reflect that on the street.

When you want to paint something, how do you go about it? How do you decide on a space or what to paint?

Nowadays I mostly participate in projects, in festivals and that kind of thing, or I get

Creating art at a friend's house

Almost complete mural for *O Bairro i o Mundo* project in Quinta do Mocho neighbourhood of Lourdes

commissioned to do work. Of course I still paint in the street, for pleasure. However a while back I was painting a lot more, pretty much every day and I would look for available spaces to paint on. This was at a time when people painted in the street in Buenos Aires, but not as much as they do now. I would always ask the neighbours' permission, this is something I always do.

Mural in Humahuaca, Jujuy

Once I have the spot, I draw a bit on some paper and then I start painting with whatever I have, the colours I have at the time A while ago it was difficult for me to buy materials to paint with, they are really expensive, so I painted with whatever I had. My style is quite free and the piece tends to change a lot from the original sketch. It is quite a freestyle process.

What projects are you working on at the moment?

I'm working on a lot of projects. One from three or four years back that is happening in Barracas, a neighbourhood here in the South of Buenos Aires. It's really beautiful and old. I'm working with a business called Sullair on a project called *Sullair Cultura*. The company is based in the neighbourhood, and with their help we are doing murals and intervening in public spaces around the neighbourhood with the permission of the residents of course. We are getting in touch with other artists. I am putting them in touch with the company, lots of them are my friends from the urban art world.

At the moment we are also creating a book called *Siete Murales*. The book talks about the first seven murals that we made in Barracas with the project, with images and focused sections on each mural. There will also be prologues from representatives of institutions such as the Universidad de Buenos Aires, and recognized art critics and anthropologists.

Also, since I moved to Barracas a couple of months ago I've been living in a house that is also a workspace. It's quite big and I'm sharing it with a friend who is a ceramics artist. I'm preparing a few projects for next year. The first one will be the presentation of the book which will take place here, and then next year I'm thinking about starting an artists' residence here for artists who paint in the street. I'm thinking of inviting them to come and live here for a few months and for them to propose some kind of intervention in the street, be it a mural or something else. Something dedicated to, and made for, the neighbourhood.

* MAY NOT REMAIN SILENT
WHOEVER WANTS TO LIVE HAPPILY...

EASY MONEY

AN UNEARTHED FILM NOIR GEM OFFERS AN ANTI-MESSAGE FOR 1960S ARGENTINA

by Jessica Sequeira

A man walks past a series of tall white planks with dollar signs painted in black and grey. By his side is his business partner, a Hungarian expatriate living in Buenos Aires. His lover, dressed in flowing white, spins, coquettes and beckons in the distance. The vague yet evocative dream of the elegance money can buy isn't concrete; we don't see fancy cars or luxury mansions. It's almost as if the newspaper reporter's vision of wealth is so unreal to him, he can't even fill in the fantasy with details. Yet its vague fairy tale elegance is tempting enough to lead him to take a number of concrete steps in his impoverished, sordid, but very real life.

The scene is part of the beautifully filmed *The Bitter Stems* (Los Tallos Amargos), a classic Argentine noir directed by Fernando Ayala and originally screened in 1956. The film was largely forgotten until an old negative was rediscovered by Argentine collector Fernando Martín Peña in a private house in Buenos Aires province. *The Bitter Stems* won Argentina's Silver Condor Award for best film of the year in 1957, and was named one of the "50 Best Photographed Films of All-Time" by Ricardo Younis of American Cinematographer in 2000. Now restored, the film is finding new viewers, having been screened in 2016 for the first time in North America as part of San Francisco's Noir City film festival and later at MoMA's *Death Is My Dance Partner: Film Noir in Postwar Argentina* season in New York. Atmospheric and gorgeous, it is set to a moody score by Astor Piazzolla, and the backdrop is classic Buenos Aires: cafés with gold cursive writing on the glass, large potted plants, tiny espressos, piano played in a minor key, bookshelves, cigarettes, curtains billowing in the wind, light falling through shutters, tango, cabaret, men in suits and ties, women in silk dresses with plunging necklines.

At first glance, the plot sounds like it could belong to any noir. Alfredo Gasper, a newspaper reporter in Buenos Aires, sets up a fraudulent correspondence school of journalism with a Hungarian expat, Par Liúdas. Lured by the promise of quick writing abilities, followed by riches and worldly success, earnest would-be reporters from across the country begin sending envelopes of money by the bushelful to the pair. Eventually, however, Gasper begins to suspect that his partner wants to edge him out of the operation, and despairing at the thought of losing all the money he has invested along with his honour, he takes action. Murder is an idea mulled over, and carried out. Piled up abstractions, clear individually, lead to a lack of control. Gasper grows paranoid, and begins to ask himself questions. What was chance and what was fate? What was planned and what was random? How much control did he really have? These were questions in the 50s, as they are now.

In *The Bitter Stems*, rather than characters with strong personalities, we find types. Liúdas and Gasper are mirror images. Both are portrayed as cynical and relatively shameless. Liúdas wants to make money to send back to his wife and two children in Europe; Gasper hopes to build a better life for himself and his woman than his meagre reporter's salary allows. Besides ambition, Gasper is also deeply neurotic and insecure, unlike the blithe and enterprising Hungarian. The camera zooms in on his face often; his moustache twitches, we see the sweat on his brow, his hands curl into fists, his jaw clenches like that of an angry little boy.

The lure of easy money: this is what makes Gasper agree to the scheme. It motivates both of the businessmen, and their clients, who want to win the title of journalist, an attractive cosmopolitan profession, without attending real classes or doing the work of writing. The correspondence school of journalism works as a scam precisely because it is driven by the desire to acquire the trappings of glamour without work. Does all of society think like this, looking for easy success and the *truco* (trick) that will vault them up the ladder? Glamour is a synonym for effortlessness, and the lubricant to make it possible is money. The goal of everyone in the movie is clear: success, respect

and riches. The only question is how to acquire them.

One rainy evening full of dramatic lightning, overwhelmed by distrust, Gasper deals his partner a deathblow on the head. He buries him in the backyard of his house, tamping down the earth with a spade. No one suspects anything or notices Liúdas is missing, until a boy turns up at the office of the 'academy'; it's Liúdas' son from overseas. Soon he falls in love with Gasper's sister. The son is ambitious too, but willing to take his time and abide by the law in making his living. He is the one who remains at the end, pointing the way toward the future. But while this innocent hope and restoration of honesty may be necessary, it involves a sacrifice: the loss of glamour. To the world-weary *porteños* of this stratum, newspapermen, cabaret dancers, small-time crooks and disenchanted lovers, the son may even seem slightly slow in the head. The terrible truth is that evil and idleness often have glamour, while solid hard work does not.

This is not a simple moral story. To get ahead, the first two want to move quickly, skipping the step of 'work'; Liúdas' son appears mentally honest but slower-paced, interested only in seeing the sights of the city and making earnest plans for his own life. Gasper and Liúdas appear to speed into losing control, while Liúdas' son keeps his hold on the reins. Yet moving quickly and unpredictably can also often operate to

personal advantage. Gasper's quick decision, made in a moment of desire to get ahead rapidly, is followed by slow burning guilt. He commits suicide, but if he had not, he would have gotten away with his act and continued to rake in the cash.

The innocence of Liudas' son and Gasper's sister don't instil confidence in the viewer. Perhaps the corrosive cynicism of the society in which he finds himself may make him a Gasper type in the future, without even the remorse. The earnest young man from Europe is not so different from the earnest provincial young men Gasper and Liúdas have been swindling. Three crimes supply the skeleton of this movie: the scam involving a fake journalism school, the brutal murder, and the partial self-hoodwinking of a gullible society.

When the film was initially released, the Peronist era had just ended. The director, Fernando Ayala, was one of several film-makers who wanted to make a more realist social cinema, distanced from successes of the previous decades such as the epic *The Gaucho War* (1942) or the militant neorealist drama *Prisoners of the Earth* (1939). The film was adapted from a book by Adolfo Jasca, which was awarded the nation's prestigious Emecé prize in 1954 (though it would not be published until 1955). Jasca wrote for a mass public, and was influenced by writers like Haroldo Conti and Héctor Oesterheld.

In the 60s the trend of literary adaptations would pick up steam in Argentina. According to film director Sergio Wolf, Leopoldo Torre Nilsson's first films, León Klimovsky's 1952 version of Ernesto Sábato's *The Tunnel* (El Túnel), and Ayala's adaptation of Adolfo Jasca's *The Bitter Stems* foreshadowed what would occur in the following decade. Prestigious directors adapted the work of well-known contemporary authors, such as Simón Feldman with his version of Osvaldo Dragún's *Those at Table Ten* (Los De La Mesa 10), Lautaro Murúa's film *Alias Gardelito* based on a story by Bernardo Kordon, and José Martínez Suárez's version of *Dar La Cara* by David Viñas. Scriptwriting adaptations, including Antonio Di Benedetto's rewriting of *Álamos Talados* (Felled Poplars) for Catrano Catrani, Julio Cortázar's co-writing of *Circe* with Manuel Antín, and Juan José Saer's *Stick and Bone* (Palo y Hueso) for Nicolás Sarquis, also introduced a new collaboration between writers and directors. This collaboration gave way in the 70s, when many film-makers began to write their own scripts or even do without scripts altogether, in a trend of improvisation during the period, influenced by surrealism and theatrical traditions, as well as the desire to challenge structure and the censorship laws of the period.

Ayala's film was shown in 1956, the year after the *Revolución Libertadora* saw a military coup end President Juan Perón's second term. While in much of the rest of the world the 50s were a golden period of increased economic prosperity, with families moving to the suburbs, acquiring household appliances, and embracing the conditions that would lead to the baby boom, in Argentina this was a time of economic stagnation and political instability. In several scenes of the film, the characters are drenched with sweat, trying to cool themselves in front of wheezing old fans in the suffocating Buenos Aires summer, dreaming of riches. The Hungarian Liúdas and the German and Italian-descended Gasper are in some sense typical characters, trying to better their circumstances by whatever means possible. Their frustration and search for the *truco* that could transform their situation was a motivation many middle class *porteños* could identify with, and low-level resignation to corruption or minor stretching of the truth to get by was widespread.

At the end of the film, Liúdas' son proclaims that he is going to dig up a plant in Gasper's back yard, in order to plant it more solidly. The plant is special; it has 'bitter stems' and will produce great fruits. His father had put it in crookedly, and he wants to set it right so it will thrive. Gasper grows very nervous, as the plant is directly in the spot where he buried Liúdas' body. He flees as the son picks up his shovel, and running to the Ituzaingó train station near the house, lies down on the tracks to meet his fate. Frantic train whistle, then cut back to the shovel, efficiently transferring dirt into a rectangle in the ground just as it did earlier in the movie. Liúdas' son is finishing the replanting. He wipes the sweat off his neck with a white handkerchief, beaming at his beautiful young girlfriend. Nothing suspect has been discovered. But just what has been buried, a new future or evidence of the scam and murder? As Piazzolla's disconcerting soundtrack strikes up, viewers are left with doubt.

ARGENTINA IS BLACK, TOO

REIMAGINING THE MAKINGS OF A NATION

by Milena Annecchiarico, Denise Braz, Prisca Gayles and Diane Ghogomu

THE BICENTENNIAL OF DENIAL

The thought that Argentina, and its golden-child Buenos Aires are European and lily-white seem to be corroborated by the faces of its world-famous football players, the Parisian facades that line its urban streets, its steak and potatoes diet, and the blaring absence of black figures identifiable in its television shows and history books. There is still a looming white cloud of misinformation and invisibilization that continues to shroud this black part of the national identity, but recently glimmers of truth about the Afro-descendents that do, indeed, inhabit Argentina, have begun to shine through. After years of tireless black activism, an increasing amount of social consciousness around African diasporic studies and the visibilization of black immigrants and their arts, Argentines are slowly witnessing the unearthing of their previously-buried African roots.

Argentines are known for taking to the streets constantly to both protest and celebrate. And over the past six years, as the young nation has consecrated a string of important anniversaries, the Afro-descendent community has taken advantage of the raucous atmosphere to make sure that their presence is known and respected. Many are rallying under the phrase 'Argentina también es Afro' ('Argentina is black too'). Though surprising for many, this expression has become increasingly pronounced amongst Afro-descendents and their activist allies. The contrarian refrain exists as a form of collective affirmation to counter the smug global mantra of 'There are no black people in Argentina'.

The series of commemorations began in 2010, during the bicentennial of the May Revolution where an unprecedented two million people took to the streets of Buenos Aires to watch more than 4,000 artists and groups perform and parade in the emblematic Plaza de Mayo. These presentations notably included communities rendered invisible by 'official' history (the Afro-descendents and indigenous people) who were united in a float called 'The Parade of Integration'. Together, with the initiative of INADI (The National Institute Against Discrimination, Xenophobia and Racism), various black organizations, artists, musicians and dancers unified in a powerful drum procession, chanting "Argentina is black, too!" And as troupes of actors re-enacted important milestones of the last two hundred years of national history, the decorated troops of enslaved Africans who fought in the Wars of Independence were finally given their just recognition in the public eye.

As Afro-descendents work to take back their space in the Argentine public-eye, it is just as important to garner proof of their presence on paper. In 2010, the national census included a measure to count Argentina's black population, a question that had been removed in 1895. This practice of statistical transference, making racial categories disappear, was one of many tactics used to 'whiten' the nation both visibly and on paper. More than 140 thousand Argentineans identified themselves as 'Afro-descendent', which is a bit less than 1% of the population. Scholars, however, estimate that the actual numbers hover around 4%, as Afro-descendents are prone to be undercounted and often do not self-identify as such due to a lack of information surrounding the terminology, and the disdain that is habitually associated with blackness. Despite the discrepancy of the figures, these numbers and acts of visualizing and recognising the Afro-community are paramount to making sure that Afro-descendents receive full protection under the law and under the government that serves them.

Thanks to the activism of black social movements of the last 20 years and joint efforts with international organizations, government institutions are finally beginning to reconstruct the history of Afro-Argentines and redefine their identity within a pluricultural framework. One of the most important movements in this direction was in the year 2013, which marked the ratification of the María Remedios del Valle Law. This law declared November 8th as the National Day of Afro-Argentines and Black Culture on the official school calendar, in honour of a black female colonel who fought in the Wars of Independence and was named 'Mother of the Nation' by General Manuel Belgrano, an Argentine Liberator.

The path to full inclusion and recognition of the cultural, civil and human rights of the black population in Argentina is still a long one. The denial of the black population currently operates on a macro-structural level (institutional racism, economic inequality, invisibility in the education system, lack of political representation, access to justice, health and media) and in the everyday experiences of black people (family concealment of black ancestors, interpersonal relationships). The 'whitening' project promulgated by the elites in the second half of the nineteenth century to create a 'modern and civilized' nation devoid of Afro-descendents and indigenous people still unconsciously or consciously colours the vision of most Argentines. Argentina consolidated its national identity by attracting European immigration at all costs, leading a genocide of indigenous people and an occupation of their land, and the acceptance of the positivist conception of capitalist progress and Eurocentric civilization. This led to the idea that Afro-Argentines had literally disappeared and that Argentina was largely white and European. But what really happened to the Afro-Argentines?

UNEARTHING BURIED TREASURE: ARGENTINA'S AFRICAN ROOTS

After the abolition of slavery, the Afro-Argentines began to disappear from the official historiography, and by the end of the 19th century the censuses stopped counting them. The Afro-Argentines who survived the civil wars and yellow fever outbreaks were pushed to the margins of a society that was more cosmopolitan and more unequal each day. At the same time, Afro-Argentine cultural practices were either isolated from what was 'authentically Argentine' or whitened and dissociated with the black community.

Despite the rampant invisibilization of the Afro population that became status quo through the 20th century, the various Afro-communities in the country have profoundly impacted Argentine culture, and they have in no way, disappeared. They were important figures in Argentina's victory during the wars of independence (1810-1825). Testimonies from travellers and paintings from the time period give us an image of a notable presence of Africans and Afro-descendents occupying all realms of social life in the major cities in the country: washerwomen, travelling merchants, construction workers, rural labourers, cobblers and artisans. They were the principal source of labour in the colonial and postcolonial era.

In fact, in cities such as Buenos Aires, Córdoba, Tucumán and Santiago del Estero, black Argentines made up 40-50% of the population. The Afro-Argentines participated and contributed actively in the cultural spaces and intellectual debates of the time period. They were the foremost composers of *milongas*, tangos, *candombes* and *payadas*, the most popular creative cultural expressions of the time. They penned black newspapers and other publications where they debated politics and human rights. They provided spaces of refuge and support for each other in their mutual aid societies and social

Photo courtesy of INADI

Photo courtesy of INADI

Photo by Denise Braz

clubs, the first ones to exist in the nation. Over the years, the diverse Afro-Argentine communities in the country continued to devise strategies of resistance based around family ties and the constant resignification of cultural practices, while bearing the weight of discrimination and invisibilization.

These days, there are more than 20 black and Afro associations in the greater Buenos Aires area. Most arose in the 1990s and 2000s and represent varied experiences from around the African diaspora: Afro descendents who trace their heritage to enslaved Africans; descendents of migrants from the islands of Cape Verde; immigrants from sub-Saharan Africa and Afro-Latinos from Uruguay, Brazil, Peru, Colombia, Haiti and Cuba, to name just a few. The first Afro-Argentine associations of the 20th century were actually founded by the Cape Verdean migrants and their Argentine-born descendents who settled to work in the port areas on the outskirts of Buenos Aires. As one of the most historically unified Afro groups in Argentina, they continue to maintain and share their heritage by hosting weekly activities as well as supporting each other's endeavours in the mutual aid societies.

Around the Argentine provinces, there are countless diverse experiences of blackness. One of the first Afro-Argentine associations, 'The Afro-Indo American House of Culture' was established in the 1980s in Santa Fe, a city that has one of the largest presences of Afro-descendents in Argentina. In Corrientes, the Afro-community continues to celebrate Saint Baltasar, the Black King of the Afro-Argentine community, and the day of the Magic Kings, every 6th of January. In Santiago del Estero, entire rural communities, such as San Felix, have identified themselves as descendents of enslaved Africans. Thankfully, these communities garnered national attention due to the 2010 census.

THE MATERIAL AND IMMATERIAL AFRICAN LEGACY

Countering and demystifying the 'disappearance' of Afro-Argentines includes resurrecting the material and immaterial legacy of Africans and their descendents in nuanced realms of Argentine culture and society. This historical excavation is incredibly important to affirming the current positive identity of Afro-Argentines. Establishing living memories and disregarding the official rumour mill that consistently associates Afro-Argentines with tragic stories of sickness, death and disappearance, ensures the acknowledgment of Afro-Argentine protagonism in the Argentine history and in the present day.

A project initiated by UNESCO in 1994, called The Slave Route, began a pluricultural research and educational project of "understanding... and underlining the interactions formed by the Transatlantic Slave Trade." Argentina was included in this project in 2009 and the UNESCO team began to identify various sites of living memory representative of Afro-descendents in Argentina. They have chosen material sites, which may be buildings or places, and immaterial sites, which may include cultural traditions and linguistic patterns, both relating to the slave trade, slavery and the post-slavery period.

The physical spaces that were chosen to give visibility to the Afro-Argentine memory were: The Chapel of the Blacks in Chascomús, in the province of Buenos Aires; The San Martin Plaza and Lezama Park in Buenos Aires; and The Jesuit Block and Missions in Córdoba. Despite the public plaques and markers, Argentina's relation with its slave past is more often than not a denied or unknown part of Argentine society. These UNESCO sites provide a rich series of educational activities which serve as pedagogical tools of communication and sensibilization that encourages the society to acknowledge its true roots.

As mentioned, The UNESCO 'memory spaces' in Buenos Aires, San Martin Plaza and Lezama Park, are places that are quite well known and well-transited by inhabitants and visitors of Buenos Aires alike. Little do most citizens know that these lands of leisure where families drink *yerba mate* and strum guitars used to be occupied by French and English slave-trading companies. After arriving in the Buenos Aires port, the enslaved Africans were brought to these spaces to be counted, weighed and, finally, sold. These establishments deteriorated, their ruins discarded, but commemorative plaques now stand as a form of consolation, recuperation and recognition. There are so many other possible sites that were important in maintaining this slave-port city, but in the rebuilding of Buenos Aires as a 'modern' city, many of these structures were quickly demolished, and along with them the legacy of the African lives brought to and bought in Argentina.

In 2012, just outside Buenos Aires, Afro-Argentine activists and their allies celebrated 150 years of the 'Chapel of the Blacks'. There was an emotional candle-lighting ceremony that featured shows by local artists, *candombe* musicians and testimonies about the history of the humble structure. The Chapel is one of the few, well-conserved material testimonies of the African presence just outside of Buenos Aires. Founded in the middle of the 19th century by the Brotherhood of Morenos, this was a place of both recreational and religious nature. Popular and syncretic religion reign as images and figurines of Catholic saints cohabitate with popular Argentine saints, historic Argentine figures and gods from Afro-American religions. La Capilla de Los Negros, as it is called, is open to all of those who want to visit and leave their offering, and is maintained by generation after generation of the black families who founded the space. It remains a gathering place and symbol of resistance for Afro-activism, where religious celebrations, artistic and political actions, still echo in the small, square site.

The Jesuit Block and the Jesuit Missions in the mountainous province of Córdoba – a 15-hour winding bus ride from Buenos Aires – are a sobering and meticulously preserved reminder of the religious order's participation in the slave trade, a fact that was squarely snuffed by the Jesuit centres until the UNESCO project claimed them in honour of black Argentine history. A visit to La Estancia Jesuitica in Córdoba's Alta Gracia exemplifies the dimensions of the cruelty of the slave system, countering those all-too-common claims that Argentine slavery was benevolent and nothing like the brutal slave systems of the USA or Brazil.

Along with the material sites, the immaterial sites of black patrimony include a group of some of the most recognisable cultural products from the city of Buenos Aires: tango, *milonga* and *payada*, along with other musical styles and traditions that are usually attributed to their black neighbours in the Rio Plata, such as *candombe* and *comparsas*.

BLACK ART RESISTS: POPULAR ARTISTIC GENRES

Afro-Americans have always contributed immensely to cultural life in the Americas, and Afro-Argentines were certainly no different. In the colonial era black people would consistently make music and dance publicly in the streets of Buenos Aires. These dances were important to unify the black community and reinforce their ethnic-cultural identities. Moreover, these black dances were strong political statements both traditionally and socially. Drumming and music was often utilized in the support of political candidates or in protests. Socially-speaking, these gatherings often faced government or police repression due to the attitudes that white society had over black gatherings. It was in the underground spaces, where Afro-Argentines mixed with European migrants, that popular genres characteristic of Argentine culture (tango and *candombe*) were born.

The first stories about *candombe* appear in the 19th century. The oldest records show that this style and rhythm of music – which includes three distinct drums, often draped over the musician's body to enable marching and dancing – were involved in the traditional parties during Easter, Christmas and, especially, carnival. The *comparsas*, groups who marched and drummed and danced, were allowed for the first time in Buenos Aires in the carnival of 1836. In this parade, the majority of the African Nations, organizations created by the Africans and Afro-Argentines, debuted their artistry. The *comparsas* boasted their own names, festive and distinctly African costumes, dancers and drummers. But by the end of the century, when the black community was greatly reduced, *candombe* began to lose its relevance in the carnival's parties to other carnivalesque practices such as *murga*.

Candombe remained as an activity practiced inside the households of Afro-Argentines, rather than in the public streets, until its return hundreds of years later, in the 1970s, with the arrival of Afro-Uruguayan immigrants escaping the military dictatorship. Recently, in the 90s *candombe* has begun to occupy more public spaces in the city, especially in the neighbourhood of San Telmo, which was called the neighbourhood of the drum, in postcolonial Buenos Aires. At the same time, *candombe*, played and maintained by Afro-Argentine families, has begun to regain visibility and garner the interest of musicians as well as researchers.

The image of tango: black tuxedos, ballrooms, sweepingly romantic but notably hip-less movements, don't immediately conjure the image of Africa. But, according to many ethnomusicologists, the tango was born from the rhythms of the Afro-Argentine practices of the *milonga* and *candombe*. You can just listen to the sound and the words of *milonga* and *candombe* to sniff out their African origin, but many don't acknowledge the fact that tango may also come from the African word, a creolization of a West African god of thunder, Shango. This remains a little-known fact in Argentina, where tango has been 'whitened' rhythmically and aesthetically as it percolated up from being a dance of the brothels to gaining popularity amongst the high-society in Paris, after which it was finally embraced as an Argentine cultural treasure.

The first tango ever registered on sheet music was "El Entrerriano" in 1897. This celebrated composition was written by the Afro-Argentine Rosendo Mendizábal. Afro-Argentines were amongst the first and most celebrated tango and *milonga* composers (Rosendo Mendizábal, Horacio Salgan, Joaquín Gabino Ezeiza). The Afro-Argentines participated actively in the cultural spaces and intellectual debates of the time, through newspapers and other publications, as well as mutual aid societies during carnival, and their celebrated *candombe* groups.

These days, reggae is a popular musical style in Buenos Aires, and Fidel Nadal is one of the genre's biggest representatives. In the 80s Fidel Nadal was part of the band Todos Tus Muertos and currently is a soloist in the band Lumumba. He is the son of Enrique Nadal, an important Afro-Argentine militant. Along with his Afro-diasporic musical references, he presents racial-ethnic ideas that have been influenced by the activist struggle of his father.

Another style of contemporary music which has maintained and incubated the Afro identity is rap. After hip-hop's birth in the late 70s in New York, it arrived in Argentina in the 1980s by way of breakdance films, such as *Wild Style*. There are two documentaries that follow this initial era. The first is called *El Juego* (1998) which depicts the initial arrival and movement of rap from the breakdance community. The recent documentary *Buenos Aires Rap* (2014) shows the pathway that rap has taken in Buenos Aires, as well as discussing other current Afro artists and the musical and cultural references within their hip-hop productions. In 2012, the civil association DIAFAR (Diaspora Africana en la Argentina) created a music video called "Rap Against Racism", in which many national and international artists sang to the world to let it know that in Argentina, rap is just as committed to the fight against racism. These productions have a strong reference from the United States in both aesthetic and artistry.

To continue with the grand commemorations of the decade, 2016 is the 100th anniversary of the death of Gabino Ezeiza, one of the greatest Argentine *payadores*, and author/interpreter of more than 500 compositions. Apart from his creative virtuosity, he was actively committed to helping the Afro-Argentine community advance politically. In the black newspaper La Juventud he wrote, "Let's contribute for all of us, so that our union is indisputable, and so that there will be legacy in the moment in which we must make practical our desire for political liberty." Though it's debatable whether Afro-descendents in Argentina have achieved the political liberty that Ezeiza yearned for, they continue to make enormous contributions to the Argentine society. But until that truth becomes self-evident to the world, we will continue to insist that 'Argentina is Black, too!'

REVOLUTIONARY COMICS

In 1968 comic book writer Héctor Germán Oesterheld worked with the artists Alberto Breccia and Enrique Breccia to publish a biography of Che Guevera. Titled *Vida del Che* the publication was a passionate homage to Guevera that was not seen favourably by the Argentine government, who removed it from circulation and destroyed all copies. Oosterheld would later write a scathing biography of Evita Perón and allegedly joined the leftist guerrilla group, the Montoneros.

Known for sci-fi comic books such as *Sargento Kirk, Bull Rocket* and *El Eternauta*, Oeserheld's last title *El Eternauta, Part II* would describe a futuristic Argentina under a dictatorship. In the same year that it was published Oesterheld went missing and it is presumed that he – along with his daughters – is among the tens of thousands of disappeared who were captured and killed by the government following the 1976 coup d'état.

Oesterheld's work keeps finding new audiences, with *El Eternauta* being published in English as *The Eternaut* in 2015.

The image to the left is a cover by Enrique Breccia for the *Vida del Che* book.

MURGA

THE RESURGENCE OF A WORKING CLASS TRADITION

by Russell Slater

Murga means many things to different people. To those outside Argentina it's perhaps best known as a staple of Uruguay's carnival, where it's performed on makeshift stages every day during carnival, which in Uruguay can last up to 40 days. In Uruguay *murga* takes on a highly-satirical bent, offering critiques of modern politics mainly using groups of singers and percussionists. It arrived in Uruguay from Cádiz in Spain when a visiting theatre group took a performance of this very particular anecdotal, mocking style of theatre onto the streets and made a big impression on the locals. Over the years Montevideo's African-descended population, largely brought over as slaves, ensured that the Uruguayans put their own spin on the custom, with clear African references emerging in the accompanying dance and dress, as well as the use of the *candombe* rhythm, which gave *murga* an extra percussive power. Together with *candombe*, *murga* is the highlight of Montevideo's carnival each year, and a great source of pride for many Uruguayans.

In Argentina the style is similar to its Uruguayan cousin but with its own definitive character. Prominent in the 1950s and 60s and then largely ignored until the 1990s it has since had a resurgence in popularity that is seeing both carnival and *murga* grow in stature in the country year on year. Its intention is the same, it has the same picaresque style that came over from Spain, as well as an affiliation with the working class, which in itself is one of the reasons why it has become such a good platform for poking fun at those in power, and especially those who are seen as corrupt. Yet it's also become its own thing. In Uruguay *murga* happens on a stage, and often people will sit to watch the performances. They then have *candombe* as a samba-esque drum and dance parade that powers through the streets. In some ways Argentine *murga* combines these two traditions. The *comparsa*, which is the name for the whole troupe, will traverse through the street. Comprised of dancers, flag-bearers and percussionists wearing sequinned, satin costumes, they will sometimes make their way to a stage for a finale or for a segment involving lyrics, but not always. Though still offering critique in the theme of the *comparsa* and in their fancy dress, there is a clear shift in Argentine *murga* from a vocal-led style to a more dance and drum-based format.

THE RISE AND FALL (AND RISE AGAIN) OF MURGA

Carnival and *murga* has a huge history across Argentina. In Buenos Aires, groups began performing *murga* as far back as the early 1900s. Later, the province of Corrientes would become notable for its carnivals from the early 1950s onwards and the tradition would be deemed a national holiday in 1956 with Argentineans being given two days off to enjoy the festivities. This stopped in 1976 when the leader of the military junta Jorge Rafael Videla struck it off the holiday list, during a period of repression. With *murga*'s ties to working class neighbourhoods and trade unions, as well as its propensity for criticising the government and those in power, it was unsurprisingly seen as a threat to those in power, and suffered a drop in popularity as a result of Videla's suppression. Some groups continued to write critical lyrics, though they would have to use metaphors and clouded language to make their point.

Unexpectedly *murga* began to make a comeback in the mid-90s. Los Auténticos Decadentes were a freewheeling ska band that emerged in the late-80s with a no-holds-barred attitude to making music and they began incorporating Afro-Latin rhythms into their music, gaining much popularity in the process. In 1992 they released "Siga El Baile", a tribute to *murga* pioneer Alberto Castillo, and then followed that up with *murga* anthem "El Murguero" in 1995. Then in 1996 *rock barrial* group Los Piojos struck big with "Verano del '92", a huge rock/pop hit with a marching *murga* beat that invaded those working class neighbourhoods once more, and ensured *murga* was back in the nation's thoughts.. What's more, the group that played drums on that record were called La Chilinga and they would themselves become one of the biggest *murga* bands in Argentina, especially in regards to recorded material.

Since then *cumbia villera* producers (such as Yerba Brava and Altos Cumbieros) have embraced *murga* rhythms as well as the more cutting-edge electronic cumbia producers, like those on ZZK Records (Chancha Vía Circuito, Tremor). On the other side of the coin Argentine and Uruguayan singer/songwriters such as Jorge Drexler, Jaime Roos, Juan Carlos Cáceres and Ariel Prat have ensured that *murga* is now well known to varied generations and classes of Argentines.

In regards to *murga* on the street you can find it in Buenos Aires neighbourhoods like Barracas, La Boca and San Telmo, as well as Corrientes, Entre Rios, Santa Fe, Jujuy and many other provinces across the country. It has now become such a national concern again that the Movimiento Nacional de Murgas (National Movement of Murgas) formed in 2000 to organise events across

Argentina, as well as helping to promote the Encuentro Nacional de Murgas (National Murga Meeting) that happens every year in Suari, Santa Fe. This resurgence has gone hand in hand with an increase in popularity for carnival celebrations, with Paso de los Libres, Monte Caseros and Gualeguaychú all having custom-built parade arenas for *murga comparsas* (intriguingly there's also a carnival specifically for samba in San Luis province each year). Confirming its rise in national popularity, the then-president Cristina Kirchner reinstated carnival's two days of national holiday in 2011, ensuring that *murga* is officially back on the agenda.

Murga illustration (opposite)
by Lee Hodges

CARNIVAL TRADITIONS

The most popular carnival in Argentina takes place in Gualeguaychú, roughly 220km north of Buenos Aires. It is notable for combining traditions from carnivals in Brazil, Uruguay and from earlier Argentine carnivals, such as those in Corrientes. Every Saturday during Argentina's summer (lasting from early January 'til the end of February) the Corsódromo (an open air parade arena, similar to Rio's Sambodrome) is alive with huge *comparsas* featuring up to 260 members, with professional floats, lavish fancy dresses and groups of dancers and drummers led by the carnival queen. Many of these *comparsas* have been going since the late 70s and early 80s when informal *murga* groups began to organise themselves and started the carnival committee. It has since become a huge attraction, with the Corsódromo being built in 1997 and now capable of hosting 35,000 people every Saturday during carnival season.

For an example of *murga*'s signature mocking style you can take a look at Los Chiflados de Boedo, a popular *murga* group in Buenos Aires. During carnival in 2016 members of the *comparsa*, with tongues firmly in cheek, dressed up as controversial figures from the Argentine press, such as TV dancing judge Marcelo Polino, dancer Victoria Xipolitakis (who was allowed to accelerate an Aerolíneas Argentinas airplane during its takeoff – the two pilots who allowed this to happen were later sacked) and the Turkish actor Ergun Demir, who has become a hugely popular figure in Argentina off the back of being in a TV dancing show. [Like in the rest of the world, it seems dancing on TV is a great way of giving your popularity a boost.]

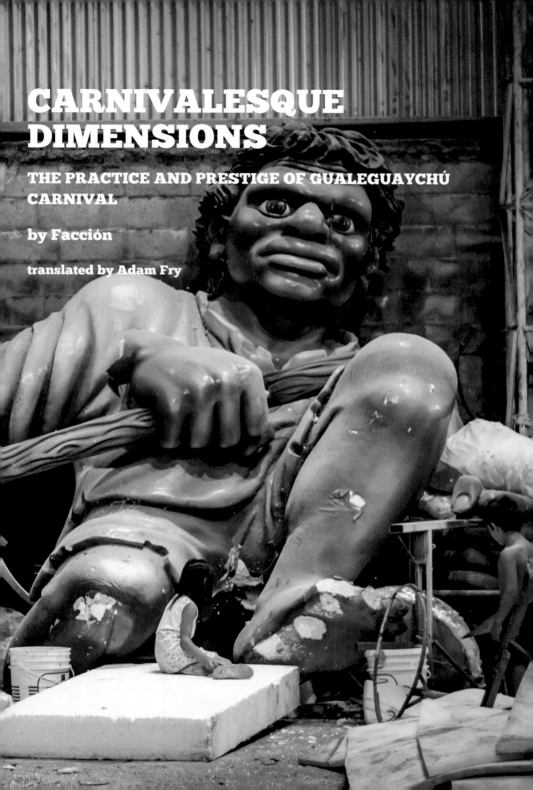

CARNIVALESQUE
DIMENSIONS

THE PRACTICE AND PRESTIGE OF GUALEGUAYCHÚ
CARNIVAL

by Facción

translated by Adam Fry

In just one reality many dimensions coexist. On one side you have the superficial, those who come and observe and live the carnival each year. On a deeper, more intimate level, you find those that create, make and dance the carnival, those who put their blood, sweat and tears on the line throughout the year in preparation for the 'desfile' or procession. An entire community, connected to a process that had previously existsedout of the limelight, is revealed in the Corsódromo each summer.

The vast majority of people that form part of the carnival family have been involved for a number of years; daughters, mothers and grandmothers dance together. This strong emotional bond mixes with the superficial expectation of the public who want to be entertained, to be swept away in the exuberance of the voluptuously-dressed bodies swaying to the rhythm of drums atop allegoric floats. For many it's an excuse to drink, look at the dancers, steal a sneaky snap and spend a night doing something a little different. Others connect to the dancing and the traditions of the spectacle.

Each *comparsa* or group's productions involve many millions of pesos, unequally distributed. From afar it's tough to spot the differences, after all, each production is wrapped up in the same luminous sheen. Behind the scenes, however, the social differences of each *comparsa* become more obvious.

Everything is blended together to form a tradition that has been maintained for many years. Even though it may be a 'touristy' carnival, the effort of those that create it is not in vain. Thanks to them, the Gualeguaychú carnival lives on, and through its beating heart a web of different carnival dimensions are woven.

LA ZAMBA

THE LOST ART OF ZAMBA AND ITS DEVELOPMENT IN ARGENTINA'S FOLKLORE SCENE

by Jacob Lassar

Visiting Argentina as a tourist, the first thing most people will tell you is how important it is to learn and dance tango. After all, isn't it THE thing to do in Argentina? The defining identity of the country known for its delicious beef steaks and red wine? A walk through many neighbourhoods of the capital, in particular the touristy area of La Boca in Buenos Aires, will reinforce a visitors' notion that tango is omnipresent and its dance must be learnt at birth by every Argentinean. Tango courses are offered at hostels, tourist agencies and restaurants alike and is almost inescapable for the foreigner. As much as this musical cliché is one of the main exports of the country, it is fascinating to look at how Argentina's folkloric culture has failed to become ingrained in the national identity as strongly as tango has, despite folklore having a stronger connection in some areas of Argentina outside of Buenos Aires. In recent years, a search for musical and cultural roots throughout South America has seen the popularity of folklore rise, particularly in the case of *zamba*, a dance and music that stands out as a symbol reflecting the history of a country driven by a strong musical identity.

***

It was a hot evening in the northern Argentine city of Salta. A blend of cumbia, tango and Argentine pop sounds filled the streets as I walked down Balcarce Street in a popular party area of the city. There was one sound in particular that caught my attention. A slow rhythmic hollow drum paired with beautiful guitar strings. It was different, profound, beautiful. It was Argentine *zamba*, played with a *bombo legüero* (an Argentine drum) and guitar and sung with a longing for love.

Zamba has nothing to do with its more famous Brazilian homophone samba. It's a folkloric dance with accompanying music popular in Argentina's rural areas, particularly in the northern provinces of Salta, Tucumán and Catamarca. Although nowadays mainly found in Argentina, *zamba* originates from the traditional *zambacueca*, an Afro-Peruvian colonial dance of the early 19th century (currently known as *marinera* in Peru). Like most Latin American music styles, *zamba* and *zambacueca* take their influences from a crossover between the music of the Amerindian *indigenas* and African music and rhythms brought into the continent by the slave trade. Through the Andean trade routes, these Afro-Amerindian musical rhythms spread along the Cordillera de los Andes, leading to the eventual establishment of the *cueca*, another well-known folklore dance and music, and the *zamba*.

When *zamba* is performed, it is nothing short of Latino-style romance. While the band plays and the singer offers up love-infused lyrics, a couple dances in gracious moves around each other, whirling a handkerchief with their hands. It seems as if every step is pre-planned, so that there is no break in eye contact. Unlike tango, the couple never touches and the focus of the audience is on the handkerchief, which plays a vital role in telling the story of the songs and symbolizes an extension of the hand wooing the partner, reinforced by the themes of melancholy, passion and longing for love, all pervasive motifs throughout Latin music. "The choreography of the dance rehearses the man's attempt to seduce his partner", says renowned musicologist and composer Alfonso Padilla. 'Las zambas' is a term dating back to colonial times and coined to identify women of Afro-Amerindian heritage. Seducing 'las zambas' is the principal objective of the dance.

Not all *zambas* are romance-related, however. In fact, one of the most well known melodies, "La Zamba de Vargas" (The Zamba of Vargas) tells the story of Felipe Varela, a federal *caudillo* (officer) who fought and lost against the military during the Argentine Civil Wars of 1867. Legend has it that during that fight the song was played by the military band and that it influenced the outcome in favour of the nationalists. Still popular to this day around Argentina, the original melody was composed by Andrés Chazarreta in 1906 and subsequently covered by *zamba* pioneers Vicente Forte, Juan Alfonso Carrizo and Los Hermanos Ábalos.

Widely considered 'the mother of all zambas', the song reflects the patriotic sentiments and attitudes of many Argentineans during the 19th century and is considered the moment in which the Argentine *zamba* was born:

> "Riojans are marshalling in Pozo de Vargas;
> Varela sends them, firm in battle,
> Against the Santiagueños, with great courage, you will fight;
> Already Don Manuel Taboada has raised his sword: it shines.

Varela attacked with great force:
Beheading, with a sword and a spear,
Cries are heard in the noise of battle,
And already the Santiagueños of Taboada are losing ground.

"Brave Santiagueños" – Taboada said-
victory or death, turn your faces.

For the beloved land, we give life to win
And right then and there, he ordered the band to play the old *zamba*."

During the era of mass immigration into Argentina (around 1880-1930), *zamba* and other folkloric dance and music styles continued to be popular and a prominent form of musical entertainment in the rural regions of Argentina, especially promoted through great folkloric musicians like Ramón Sixto Ríos (who composed the hugely-popular folk song "Merceditas"), Jorge Cafrune (composer of "Zamba de Mi Esperanza"), Carlos Guastavino and Polo Gimenez. Meanwhile, the various immigration waves from the late 1890s until the 1950s, mainly from Europe and mostly Italians, led Argentina to experience a demographic shift, which in turn influenced popular music in the country.

In the cities of Buenos Aires, Córdoba and Santa Fe many Italian immigrants settled and fused the slow and melancholic rhythms and dances of *zambacueca* and other folkloric music with their Italian musical background, eventually leading to the formation of tango. Whilst tango initially grew out of the working class neighbourhoods, it went on to be seen by many as the dance of 'urban citizens'. Music historian Julie Taylor even notes it was taken up by the 'bourgeoisie' as an emblem of national identity. For some decades after, folklore remained isolated in rural areas, played only at local fairs and festivals. During the 1960s and 70s however, artists such as Mercedes Sosa and Atahualpa Yupanqui emerged thanks to the folklore boom experienced by the entire South American continent, in a movement known as *nueva canción*. 'Going back to the roots' became popular all across South America, and so did folkloric styles such as *zamba*. Los Trovadores, Cuarteto Zupuy and Los Chalchaleros, all infamous traditional Argentine folklore musicians, started to perform in the urban centres and gained leverage as symbols of Argentina's national identity.

Though tango may always have its place as the 'national' music of Argentina, Argentine folklore is finding its way back to its former glory through art and music festivals and a renewed 'back to the roots' spirit. Cultural institutions across Argentina are increasingly featuring *zamba* performances, schools in the northern provinces of Jujuy, Santiago del Estero and Tucumán are organizing folkloric dancing competitions and documentaries such as *Argentina* by well-known Spanish director Carlos Saura capture the cultural, musical and expressionist relevance of *zamba* and other folklore, telling the story of Argentina and promoting the beauty of the dances. The yearly Festival Nacional de la Zamba en Tucumán and other similar folklore events keep the spirit of Argentina's origins alive and enable locals and visitors alike to enjoy the beauty of *zamba*.

FESTIVAL OF FOLKLORE
by JACOB LASSAR

Nestled within the scenic Valle de Punilla in Córdoba, at the feet of the imposing cross-embellished Cerro Pan de Azúcar, lies Cosquín. For most of the year it is an undisturbed tranquil town, attracting a small number of tourists as a health and healing retreat. But since 1961 it has been at the centre of Argentine folklore as the host of Cosquín Festival de Folklore, one of the most renowned and important folk events in Latin America.

Dedicated entirely to the artistic expression of folklore, the 9-day festival, which happens every January, offers traditional dance, food and songs from rural areas across Argentina. Searching for ways to promote tourism and the local economy, the festival originated in 1960 when a group of engaged Cosquín citizens gathered together to organize an event that would bring traditional Argentine music, dance and poetry to a wider audience. They did not however expect to attract such prestigious names as Los Chalchaleros, Horacio Guarany, Ismael Gómez or Hilda Ruffo to come to the first edition in 1961. The second festival would be broadcast live via Radio Belgrano in Buenos Aires, enabling millions of Argentineans – many of whom in the capital were still completely enthrall to tango – to become aware of the festival.

Its main acts over the years have included popular artists such as Soledad Pastorutti, Victor Heredia, León Gieco and up until his death, the renowned Argentine guitarist, poet, singer and writer Atahualpa Yupanqui. His yearly commitment and legendary status in Argentina resulted in the main stage being named after the late star. Cosquín Festival has not only attracted the greats of the Latin American folklore scene, but has also acted as a proving ground for now well-known artists. One of those was Mercedes Sosa, who later spearheaded the *nueva canción* movement of the 1970s and 80s but first came to the nation's attention at Cosquín in 1965, and would perform regularly at the festival thereafter.

Visitors can not only experience great acts on the main stage. Each year, the Congreso del Hombre Argentino y su Cultura (Congress of the Argentine Man and his Culture) accompanies the main festival where people can learn and share their experiences by taking part in singing and dancing workshops, and by buying artisanal works. Indigenous language courses in Quechua and Guarani can also be found.

The popularity of Argentine folklore has not even been constrained to Latin America. When in 1975 the first Cosquín en Japón festival took place in Kawamata, Japan, nobody would have thought it would go on to become the biggest Latin folklore festival in Asia.

Back home in Argentina, the festival keeps on growing, in significance and in size, sticking close to the principles of promoting national folkloric music that it started all the way back in the 60s.

TALES FROM THE PLAINS

CARLOS SORÍN DISCUSSES HIS FILMS, PAYING TRIBUTE TO THE PEOPLE AND LANDSCAPES OF PATAGONIA

by Stephanie Kennedy

It's winter, yet the darker nights have made the atmosphere inside the Ritzy cinema café in Brixton, South London all the more warm and fuzzy. Lively chatter, endless flows of tea, cake and wine, tables packed both upstairs and down set the scene for my meeting with Carlos Sorín. I fear the room's noise will drown out our voices on my recorder, but a small corner has been set aside for us, allowing for an intimate interview with one of Argentina's most acclaimed film directors and screenwriters. "Everyone is mad!" Sorín laughs, but you can tell he's enjoying the buzz.

As part of London's Argentine Film Festival, audiences were introduced to two of Sorín's films; *Historias Mínimas* (2002) and *Bombón El Perro* (2004). Neither films are recent but their heartfelt message from the depths of the wild and extensive plains of Patagonia in southern Argentina is as relevant today as it was when the films were first released. "The area hasn't changed, if anything, it is even less populated now", Sorín explains, "and the kind of people you meet in the films are still there". In both, the protagonists come from the same small rural town, the dusty and quiet Fitz Roy. But a momentous trip is undertaken and we follow our heroes across hundreds of kilometres, stopping at occasional service stations, shops and small eateries along the way. "In Patagonia, you can drive for 800 kilometres without seeing anyone, and so any story that happens there is inevitably tied to a journey. For the locals, travelling is quite a normal affair". The films' characters are generally cheerful but their good spirit is ridden with a sense of unease, their contentment shadowed by a deeper yearning for change. But this longing Sorín insists, is not exceptional. "Everyone goes looking for something, which I believe is intrinsic to the human condition. The old man in *Historias Mínimas* is trying to resolve some guilt he has, the man with the cake is looking for happiness and in *Bombón El Perro*, the protagonist is hoping to start his life again after losing his job". Their encounters with strangers along the way, albeit slightly awkward at first, soon turn warm and tender, and the audience is soothed by the characters' humility, their gentle words and good will. "The people of Patagonia are very reserved because they are not used to meeting other people with as much frequency as you would in the city. There, to meet someone is truly an event. But if you start to get to know them, you realize how much they look out for one another".

Carlos Sorín's interest in Patagonia stems from his own personal experience of living there. He discovered the area whilst completing his military service and found the place "terrible!" Sorín chuckles as he confirms this first impression of his; "Yes, I hated it, as soon as I got there! You have to get used to the sound of the wind 24 hours a day and it is unforgiving". Nonetheless, Sorín remained in the area and soon started to see the charm beyond the unwelcoming winds. "Those long roads, the petrol stations and hotels in the middle of nowhere, these images really intrigued me and I understood that for the locals, they were important hubs of life. I wanted to portray the immensity of this grand yet aggressive land, the open and extensive skies; the type of landscape fit for heroes and epic tales, but then contrast them with small intimate stories, simple daily life".

He shot his first film, *La Película Del Rey*, in 1986, bringing his love affair with Patagonia to the big screen. The film was based on the real life character of French lawyer, Orélie Antoine de Tounens, who arrived in Chile in 1858. Tounens picked up Mapuche, the local indigenous language, and mobilized the communities into fighting for an independent Mapuche state. Although his efforts were deemed noble by some, Tounens' alterior motive was to create a country he denominated as the New France, a mission eventually thwarted by the French state itself, which dismissed both Tounens' character and his efforts as insane. Before being condemned to an asylum and later deported back to France, Tounens became a local hero and was crowned 'King of Patagonia'. It is a curious story, one akin to the likes of a young Sorín who remained in Patagonia to shoot his film, a venture tested by an endless chain of technical difficulties, logistical obstacles and second-rate actors, until the associated production company eventually dropped out of the project, leaving Sorín on the brink of financial ruin.

Still, the film survived and it was released three years after Argentina's military dictatorship had fallen. At the time, art, culture and cinema inevitably turned to the documentation of the country's recent political history, as a people desperately tried to grapple with what had just happened to them. "The regime and the forced disappearances is a theme that cannot be exhausted. At the time, most if not all films looked at this issue and I believe there are still many more films about this that could be made". Yet *La Película Del Rey* spoke of something completely different, depicting wild and beautiful countryside with simple characters and their magnificent plans. It struck a chord with Argentineans. "I think the film offered the audiences of the time a glimpse of a remote Argentina, one that looked stuck in the 1930s, the country of their childhood. It portrayed innocence and it was appreciated with a deep sense of nostalgia, as many thought back to an Argentina of before the war."

The public's gradual idealization of Patagonia was a welcome turn, as the area had been abandoned and neglected for many years. A petrol boom mid 20th century had scattered oil refineries across the landscape, but the desert stretches and lonely winds visualised by Sorín's films remained largely unperturbed. Nonetheless, the search for oil had contributed to a growing national interest in the area, leading to many Argentineans' rediscovery of Patagonia. They were drawn to the western regions, another type of landscape all together and very different from Sorín's east. It is an area of spectacular natural beauty, lined by the jagged range of the Andes; a staggering

immensity only interrupted by the pristine turquoise lakes that slow you down to take in the earth's saw-toothed heights. Western Patagonia became a hotspot for young people and ex-hippies, and soon, the word spread that Patagonia was a paradise. "At the time in Buenos Aires, everyone was talking about leaving their job in the city and escaping to Patagonia; 'I'm going to give it all up and live in a cabin'", Sorín explains by mimicking a particularly common type of character we probably could all identify. "It was a plan very few actually carried out yet this trend fostered a general impression of Patagonia; one of romantic mysticism". According to Sorín, Patagonia's expanse was thus considered not only as a reserve of natural resources, but also as a "moral reserve"; a place where life was still simple and a welcoming refuge from modernity. "This analysis is of course incomplete," I am reminded as Sorín shakes his head in dis-approval of an easy stereotype, "but it was the fashionable opinion from Buenos Aires".

As Argentina's appreciation for Patagonia continued to develop, so did its political concerns. Economic rivalry with Chile meant that the area it shared with its neighbour became a point of comparison and competition, the border running through South America's tip like a measuring tape. It continues to be a point of antagonism between the two countries, who each claim the area to be originally and in its entirety theirs. A trip to the border reveals the Chilean side as a long thread of grand hotels and imposing infrastructure, whereas Argentina's side is relatively barren. "They've stolen our Patagonia!" Carlos chuckles again, as he relays what appears to be a common Argentine lament.

The 1980s saw Patagonia fitted with a new mould, a new purpose. This time, it was called upon by the nation state to serve its part in the Falklands war and its ports were transformed into military bases, a strategic manoeuvre but also an historical one; Argentineans continue to insist the Falkland Islands belong to Patagonia. Now, the mining companies have brought a fresh round of controversy to the area and Patagonia often appears on the newspapers' front pages, but for all the wrong reasons. Nonetheless, the area continues to convey a sense of mystique for many Argentineans and to this day, it remains largely unknown and underdeveloped.

I wonder out loud if Patagonians suffer any discrimination when they visit the bigger cities or try to integrate with the urban hubs. "No, no." Sorin leans sideways and clocks his head, like a firm but patient teacher. "Patagonians look like anyone and come from everywhere." He runs me through the most important migrations to the area; all relatively recent compared to the northern provinces of the country whose population is several centuries old. We discuss the significant Welsh diaspora, the Scottish and German shepherds who, at a later date, appeared in the form of oil entrepreneurs, and then of course the innumerable internal migrations, making up a body of people with no specific characteristics, of no specific colour. "But one defining trait the Patagonians do share is that they always think they are in Patagonia because they are just passing by, that they will only be there for a short while before moving on. But they always stay. It has changed slightly now, but when I was first there I noticed how the construction of their houses was often incomplete. There was always a wall or parts of the roof missing, as if to confirm their intention in the area was only temporary. However their cars and trucks were always big and powerful, because travelling and moving on was their apparent priority. People thought they would leave after the petrol boom but they have all stayed on".

I ask Sorín where else he'd like to go to shoot a film and he draws closer, eyes lighting up, as if about to share a deliciously singular secret. He asks me for my name, obviously not having heard it well the first time. "Stephanie", I tell him. "Like my daughter!" he exclaims and I feel like I'm right in the middle of Patagonia, sharing the traditional *mate* drink with the old man from *Historias Mínimas*. "Did you know that this year and last, in some rural villages of Argentina, communities have started to take justice into their own hands? I heard recently about a very poor family of which one member was an ex-convict, who had moved to the outskirts of a small town. When the rest of the community got wind of this, they went over to the poor family's house and burned it down, acting in frenzy like a pack of hounds. And because this anger, this act of retribution was spurned on by mass mentality, there was no leader and no one was held responsible. It's an expression of fascism but a curious phenomenon because it has started to happen only recently and it involves simple, normal people, like those from *Historias Mínimas*. Some of these cases end terribly, with people beaten to death. It's not an easy theme, I don't know how to approach it yet". Sorín's assistant sits nearby, listening eagerly. I want to stay and hear more of the story but I look at my watch and realize my time is up. I thank them both before Sorín gets up and asks for half a cup of warm milk, his small frame suddenly jostled about by the hustle and bustle of the bar. He smiles patiently, like a seasoned Patagonian, caught up in the wind.

PATAGONIAN TALES

THE INSPIRATION OF ARGENTINA'S SOUTHERN WILDERNESS ON CESAR AIRA

by Adam Fry

"In a small town in Argentina, a seamstress is sewing a wedding dress. All of a sudden she fears that her son has been kidnapped and driven off to Patagonia. She gives chase in a taxi. Her husband finds out and takes off after her – to the end of the world, to the place where monsters are born, and to where the southern wind falls hopelessly in love."

There can be no finer canvas upon which to paint the portrait of a nation than Patagonia. Wide, open, windy, beautifully inhospitable, it speaks of man's desire, and love, for the domination of his territory. Planting the flag in the furthermost reaches of the landscape and declaring it his homeland, his nation, his property. It is, to this day, a land that stubbornly resists the destructive whims of man. Be it mountains, winds or insects, the Argentine Patagonia, like a particularly rowdy stallion, evades taming. Part of its potential for discomfort lies in the fluidness of its boundaries. Early arrivals would mark the dimensions of their lands by how far they could see, and *estancias* became small states where livestock outnumbered humans by many thousand to one. Fickle to the smallest detail, it is a landscape to be respected from afar, and to be endured up close.

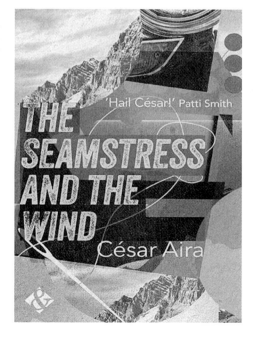

It is into this backdrop that Cesar Aira sets *The Seamstress and the Wind*. This self declared 'small boy' from Coronel Pringles, a neither-here-nor-there town on the outskirts of Buenos Aires, where bouts of gossip break up the nothingness, is one of Argentina's most prolific writers. To describe an Aira novel is to describe a snowflake. Streams of consciousness run rings around the reader, leading him or her breathlessly across pages that seem too small to contain the curious inventiveness of the writer. His literary output is prodigious, his current portfolio of novels and novellas runs to around 70, and it is said he never looks back at each page he writes, preferring to trust his instinct and creative furore as he steers each new journey.

Aira's upbringing in Coronel Pringles forms the basis for this story, set during the disappearance of his childhood friend, Omar. Pringles, a small town caught between the big city of Buenos Aires to the north and the even bigger Patagonian plains to the south, is the unspectacular starting point for the adventure, but we are quickly taken along winding roads, hurtling along with the narrative away from the humdrum of provinciality and towards windswept plateaus. We step into a world where infantile storytelling meets folk legend, seasoned heavily with tongue in cheek nods to the importance of Patagonia in the Argentine national psyche. In these open lands of Martin Fierro and solitary gauchos charged with thousands of head of livestock, Aira allows the epic to become comic, for the 'great gray plateau', so often romanticised in the mind of the claustrophobic *porteño*, to reveal itself for what it is; a darn good place in which to set a story.

Aira recalls his childhood, yet leaves us ambiguous as to where truth ends and fable begins. The perfect technique, clearly, for the vast landscape upon which the story is played out. Aira, who lived in Pringles, Buenos Aires province, until he was 18, is a writer for whom the liquidity of the Patagonian landscape is not only attractive, but fundamental to his growing up process. His place was one bordered not just by the difference to the big city, but also by the relative sense of community when compared to the utter solitude of yet more isolated settlements. Coronel Pringles is not Patagonia, but it exists, out there, on the border, in the mind of every bored villager who dreams of escaping.

Characters driven semi-mad by the maniacal wind chase each other across the plains, all searching for each other in a pointless game of tag. Omar, the young boy who supposedly disappears, becomes the focal point around which the provincial desire for something, anything, to happen are realised. The darkness of this boredom, the insipid cruelty of those with nothing to do, is explored in tragi-comedic wit. Because alongside the gaucho, lone steward of this inhospitable lands, the Argentine Patagonia speaks of pillage, displacement and murder. In the 1870s a mandate from Julio Argentino Roca swept up natives in a forced removal from their ancestral lands, a process known as the Conquest of the Desert. The state building process was undertaken by European immigrants keen to become landowners and to bring 'enlightenment' to this barren frontier. Survival was not guaranteed, but thousands of hectares were the prize for those willing to take the risk.

The demented ramblings of the eponymous

seamstress, Delia Siffoni, become a tale through which this landscape morphs into the fears, desires and urges of its inhabitants. The wilderness is at times comforting, at times terrifying. One can find solace in the silence, or utter despair in the prison of their own mind. The geography, unlike that of the city, is monotonously open, and it is the very same openness that oppresses. Roads lead one way, and the irony of its epic proportions and its parochialism is not lost on Aira. These characters are tiny specks on an enormous map where distances are continuously shortened by family tradition, stuffy idiosyncrasy and the ubiquitous *chisme*, or gossip.

Their lives are lived with the knowledge of distances that would make a city dweller shudder, and are adapted accordingly. It is not for nothing that any green behind the ears visitor to Patagonia fretting about timetables will hear "He who hurries in Patagonia, wastes time" from a wizened (or maybe accepting of his fate) local. Time, both in Patagonia and in Aira's work, is useless. The scenes he creates are timeless, peppered with references that make this an unmistakably Argentine story ("any traveller in Argentina knows that where truck drivers stop, one eats well; therefore, one stops") yet maintaining the knowing aloofness that we require him to have if we are to suspend our belief as often as he would desire.

Because this is a story that forces us into a reconsideration of our own nature. The wind, about the most dependable thing down in Patagonia, becomes a love-struck teen blowing to the whim of the frenzied seamstress. His capricious desire to be loved by Siffoni, a decidedly ordinary housewife is either laughably tragic or tenderly unfulfilled. Truck drivers gamble away their livelihoods, homes and wives in the search for excitement. Yet one cannot deny that this is also a beautifully written ode to the place Aira clearly loves. If at times it rattles along at a vertiginous pace, there is also contemplation of the beauty, of a "Patagonia, whole and limitless". It was, as he writes "a plateau as white as the moon, under a black sky filled with stars. Too big, too beautiful, to be taken in with a single gaze; and yet it must be, because no one has two gazes".

Aira's Patagonia becomes the unreachable, unimaginable panorama that it has always been in the minds of the Argentine people, a place that gives him the freedom to fly alongside his characters and to control the only thing uncontrollable, the wind itself.

The Seamstress and the Wind was originally published in Spanish as La Costura y El Viento in 1994. The English edition, published by New Directions and translated by Rosalie Knecht, was released in 2011. Other Cesar Aira publications translated into English include How I Became a Nun, The Literary Conference and Ghosts.

TESTAMENTS TO SOLITUDE

LUCAS BRIDGES' LEGACY OF PATAGONIAN RESILIENCE

words and photos by Adam Fry

The Argentina-Chile border, large, stretched and oft redrawn, has its fair share of tales. Few men have entwined their legacy so closely to this border as Lucas Bridges. An Anglo-Argentine author, explorer and rancher born in 1874 in Ushuaia, Bridges combined an intimate knowledge of the land with a unwavering support for the indigenous population of Patagonia. His exploits led the Chilean government to offer him the concession of the Baker ranch, an enormous 500,000 hectare ranch only accessible through the Argentine border and hemmed in by mountains on all sides.

Herding thousands of livestock through the Paso Roballos point, Bridges was tasked with the job of establishing a permanent human presence on behalf of the Chilean government in land unmapped and unsurveyed. A tactic that would ensure economic success and national security led by one of its hardiest adopted sons. The military runway that still exists here is proof of the strategic importance of this valley, and a modern day validation of Bridge's efforts.

Bridges and his team left behind these beautiful, desolate testaments to their daily struggle. Structures that are utilitarian, sparse, modest in scope and ridiculous in comparison to the vastness of their environs. These portraits capture these structures in their present form, some ravaged by the effect of an unforgiving climate, and some used to this day by the hardy gaucho population that follow in Bridge's footsteps. The book *Uttermost Part of the Earth* is Lucas Bridge's classic account of a life lived around the Argentine Patagonia.

The intricately tiled walls of this shack
reflect the *tejuela* styling that is common to
Patagonian houses.

The buildings, which now form part of the Parque Patagonia national park, hide secrets and surprises. Yellowed copies of the Buenos Aires Herald were found lining the walls of this hut.

Some structures are still used, and show the ingenuity of their (temporary) residents. Simple wood burners and radio masts speak of solitude and resilience.

The outposts lie dotted around this enormous stretch of land where hundreds of thousands of sheep once grazed. Riding a trusted steed, small teams of gauchos would shepherd herds through mountainous passes to virgin grassland pastures.

Don Daniel works as a *huemul* (small native deer) tracker and park ranger. His knowledge, skills and dedication allow these elusive animals to feel protected, and to ensure that the restoration of their ideal Southern Beech-rich habitat takes place.

Cerro Lucas Bridges is the emblematic peak that towers over the border crossing. So named because Bridges scaled it three times, it today bears witness to breeding populations of condors, pumas and guanaco.

Don Jose occupies the post closest to the Paso Roballos border point. A sheep farmer at heart, he grew up listening to stories of 'el ingles' who forged a path through the mountains. He lives alone, and can spend up to 200 days a year in solitude working the last remaining sheep.

FINDING FEMINA

PATAGONIA'S ALL-FEMALE FOLK/HIP-HOP TRIO

by Charis McGowan

Fémina are Clara "Wewi" Trucco (vocals, percussion), Sofia "Toti" Trucco (vocals, guitar) and Clara Miglioli (vocals), an all-female rap/folk trio hailing from San Martín de Los Andes in Argentina's Patagonia. Given the remote, rustic location of their picturesque hometown, you'd be forgiven for assuming their music is chiefly folk-orientated. Granted, their sound combines seraphic vocal harmonies with folkloric melody, yet Fémina's sound is surprisingly urban.

"We grew up listening to urban music; lots of people listen to it in San Martín. There are loads of musicians and artists there, of all different disciplines. It's a small town but there have always been great musicians around," explains Clara. "It's a very creative place."

Their enigmatic and versatile sound can be described as a fusion of rap, reggae and hip hop combined with sounds typical of South America: cumbia, *candombe*, *chacarera*, samba, bolero. While their music is shaped by regional influences, they depart from sounding characteristically Argentinean, which is broadly grounded in rock and alternative styles.

"Argentina is known for its rock, but none of us really listen to rock music!" says Wewi.

"We always liked R 'n' B, funk, soul, jazz, rap," answers Clara when asked how the girls crafted their current sound. "We started to make music but didn't know exactly what sound we wanted to make. We started with the bass and sound system. When we began to add instruments all the influences began to mix together, but it was almost by accident, it wasn't premeditated."

We are conducting the interview over Skype as Clara and Toti are currently based in

San Martín, while Wewi is in Buenos Aires. Given that there is over 1,000km of distance between them, it must be difficult to find time to come together and make music.

"We are a family: the girls are sisters and I've been a close friend since we were children" says Clara. "When we are together it can be difficult to concentrate as we have such an intimate connection that goes even beyond the music. So, perhaps the distance can help us be more organized, creatively, so that when we are together we can focus on what we have to do. In this sense, maybe working in different places won't be harder to make music, but easier."

The band recorded their first album *Deshice De Mi* in 2011, and the follow up *Traspasa* in 2014. In between independent projects and separate careers, they are working on songs for their third album. Does recording between Buenos Aires and San Martín affect their creativity?

"I think that our art is very connected to the landscape (of Patagonia)" says Clara. "Fémina has a lot of images and landscape in the lyrics and melodies, but also we connect very much with the street music and culture."

"Patagonia of course is such an inspiring place," reflects Wewi. "But here in Buenos Aires there are different types of music, more people... more movement. They are both inspirational places, but in different ways."

"We always record in Buenos Aires as it is a natural step for Argentine musicians to go there. As Wewi said, it's a place that has a lot to absorb," Clara continues. "Culturally, Buenos Aires is very developed and interesting, which makes it a suitable place to develop any artistry."

While *Deshice De Mi* and *Traspasa* were recorded independently without much input outside the three band members, the band hope to find a producer who can steer their sound into new territory, "...the first two albums we recorded were just us playing our instruments; they didn't have many digital features," says Clara.

"We would like to find someone who can capture exactly what we are looking for, which is complicated as what we want to do is broad..." continues Wewi. "We need someone who can help us to record all these ideas that we have."

It is clear that all three members put creativity at the heart of their music and art, and the direction of their third album promises to build upon the band's ingenuity in combining a variety of sounds and styles.

"With the next album we want to mix more digital sounds with the acoustics that we already have when we perform live" says Clara. "We want the new material to incorporate more hip hop, trip hop, soul... to sound more urban."

"What we want to do is broad; it is very multifaceted", Wewi continues. "...everything that we do has different sides."

BORGES' ARGENTINE TALES

In 1979 Jorge Luis Borges was asked if he would like to start compiling his Library of Babel, an idea that he had set forth in a short story collection, *El Jardín de Senderos Que Se Bifurcan* (The Garden of Forking Paths) in 1941. That tale, "The Library of Babel", spoke of a universe in which exists four bookshelves containing books that have been composed using random sequences of words. As the number of books and the sequences are infinite, this means that somewhere within those shelves are all the important books ever written, except they're surrounded by hundreds (maybe even thousands, or millions) of books containing pure gibberish. In every sense this is a story echoing the infinite monkey theorem.

Borges compiled 33 volumes for The Library of Babel that were published throughout the 80s. Each one contained a collection of stories or a single story as chosen by Borges. Amongst the volumes are collections devoted to H.G. Wells, Franz Kafka, Jack London and Oscar Wilde. Volume 30, published in 1986, contained a selection of stories by Argentine authors, titled *Cuentos Argentinos* (Argentine Tales). Containing stories by famed authors such as Adolfo Bioy Casares and Julio Cortázar as well as the lesser-known names of María Esther Vázquez and Federico Peltzer the collection offers an interesting introduction into Argentine literature. Here are the stories he chose for that anthology:

- "Prólogo (Cuentos Argentinos)" by Jorge Luis Borges (1986)
- "Yzur" by Leopoldo Lugones (1906)
- "El Calamar Opta Por Su Tinta" by Adolfo Bioy Casares (1962)
- "El Destino es Chambón" by Arturo Cancela Pilar de Lusarreta (1940)
- "Casa Tomada" by Julio Cortázar (1946)
- "La Galera" by Manuel Mujica Láinez (1951)
- "Los Objetos" by Silvina Ocampo (1959)
- "El Profesor de Ajedrez" by Federico Peltzer (1973)
- "Pudo Haberme Ocurrido" by Manuel Peyrou (1960)
- "El Elegido" by María Esther Vázquez (Unknown Date)

NB: In 2015 US author and programmer Jonathan Basile created an online version of The Library of Babel using Borges' initial concept. You can view his site at libraryofbabel. info – good luck finding that masterpiece within the incessant randomness.

EVERYTHING IS RELATED

THE IMAGINATIONAL ILLUSTRATIONS OF CLARA 'WEWI' TRUCCO

by Russell Slater

As one third of Fémina, Clara Trucco is a musician responsible for fusing elements of Patagonian folk music and culture with hip-hop and the borderless musical spirit of Manu Chao. She is also an extraordinary illustrator responsible for the aesthetic of the band, with her illustration adorning the cover of their last album *Traspasa* as well as countless gig posters. Visually, these images step away from the often urban setting of Fémina's music to a wonderland preoccupied with her Patagonian upbringing as well as a love of magic, native traditions and symbolism that's reflected in her stylized visions of characters and landscapes. Her illustrations, which have also been created for other bands and gigs as well as personal projects, transport us to a world between the real and the imagined, a hinterland occupied by indigenous gods, lost fairy tales and the common man trapped in wonderment.

What follows are a selection of Clara's illustrations as well as excerpts from our interview, where we discussed her inspiration, interests, working practice and growing up in Patagonia.

Clara's Cultural Recommendations
An image: Lanín volcano
An album: *Musica Negra* by Michael Mike
A poet: Roberto Juarroz
A film director: Leonardo Fabio

"I was born in San Martin de los Andes, a very small city in Neuquén, Patagonia. It's surrounded by beautiful landscapes, lakes and mountains, a natural dream. It's the land of the Mapuches, who were originally from there. I grew up there, having a very beautiful childhood, really magical."

"I think that most of my interests come from the place I grew up in. Living between mountains and surrounded by nature gives you a perspective of immensity. I'm interested in the mystery of universe, the continuous mutation of forms, the characters we adopt and build ourselves. Everything is related and connected."

"In a way, I've always been training as an artist. I have had many masters who have taught me and introduced me to expressions from around the world. Teachers and friends, as well as music, images and books were my guides. When I finished my studies I began to study visual arts at the university, but I didn't last too long. It was a lot of time to dedicate and I was really interested in music too."

"When I was a kid I loved to draw. I would wake up really early and I would draw for hours in complete silence. I loved creating characters.

Making a list of the artists who influenced me, would take a lifetime, but I can say that recently I've been very excited by (Jean Giraud) Moebius and (Ivan) Bilibin, two great illustrators!"

OLDER THAN BORDERS

THE CULTURE AND HISTORY OF ARGENTINA'S NATIVE PEOPLE, AND THEIR CONTINUED SEARCH FOR RECOGNITION

by Pablo Andrés Bobadilla

"We're not Indians and we're not Native Americans. We're older than both concepts. We're the people, we're the human beings", said the Santee Dakota poet and activist Jhon Trudell. His words suit every one of Americas' first nations. Before Lionel Messi, Diego Maradona, Ernesto 'Che' Guevara, Eva Perón, Jorge Luis Borges and Carlos Gardel, and long before oil, *yerba mate* and beef built Argentina's reputation, native people created culture for over 12,000 years in the lands that we now call Argentina, before the country got its name as a result of the Spanish' desire to find Potosí's silver mines (*argentum* being Latin for silver).

According to the Argentine government there are 32 pre-existing native nations, whose collective names are far less famous than those listed above: Atacama, Ava Guaraní , Aymara, Chorote, Chané Charrúa, Chulupí, Comechingón, Diaguita/Diaguita Calchaquí, Guaraní, Huarpe, Kolla, Lule Vilela, Mapuche, Mbyá Guaraní, Mocoví, Ocloya, Omaguaca, Pampa, Pilagá Quechua, Querandí, Rankulche, Sanavirón Selk'Nam (Ona), Tapiete Tehuelche, Tilián Toba, Tonocote, Tupí Guaraní and Wichí.

INVISIBILIZATION

People are not numbers, but let's pay attention to some data. The official census does not reflect the number of people who descend from Argentina's native population. The 2001 census only counted the households where indigenous people lived, not the number of people themselves, so we have to look at data from the Complementary Survey of Indigenous Peoples, which was carried out in 2004-2005 by INDEC. Based on this survey, the Economic Commission for Latin America and the Caribbean (ECLAC) published figures in 2010 that stated:

• total population of Argentina is 40,117,096;
• total indigenous population is 955,032, which is 2.4% of the total;
• the Mapuche nation is the most populous indigenous group with 113,680 people, representing 18.8% of the indigenous population.

Juan Namuncurá, member of the Mapuche dynasty Kurá Kurá, president of the Instituto de Cultura Indígena Argentina (ICIA) and founder of the political party Pueblos de la

Madre Tierra, estimates that there are 1,000,000 Mapuche and Mapuche-descendent people and that the indigenous population should be around 30% of the total population of Argentina.

"The hardest battle is to set the fact that native people are not extinct, we are not dinosaurs. We keep our past alive, remembering the genocide against us and working in the present for a better collective future", says Namuncurá, adding: "We need that Argentina follow convention 169 of the International Labour Organization (ILO) and recognize fully the rights of native people and include us in discussions regarding the use of natural resources and land".

MONEY TALKS

The 100 peso note that shows Julio Argentino Roca's face on the front has this to say about him on the back: "Soldier and statesman, organiser of the Conquest of the Desert, signed the Boundary Treaty with Chile, twice President of Argentina." Many investigators remark that it is not possible to conquer the desert and that this sentence denies the existence of indigenous people. "The state was built on genocide" says the Anthropologist Diana Lenton, member of the Research Network on Genocide. In an interview published in the newspaper Pagina /12 she argues: "There were previous military campaigns, but Roca's was the most systematic and had a more avowedly genocidal goal. There are Roca's statements about destroying everything until the last Indian. His inauguration speech as president celebrates that not a single Indian crossed the pampas. Some have the image of a romantic style of battle, with one army against another, yet the feature of that campaign was that Roca was mainly aiming at the civilian population. The memories of Army Major Prado clearly say that the attacks on the *tolderías* [*tolderías* are Mapuche villages] were planned with women and children as targets, and happened when men were not in the villages. The plan was to take the loot, especially livestock, as well as family members because that was the one thing that would lead the Indians to surrender. These are clearly actions against civilians, where women and children died, and where others were sent as slaves to do domestic work or urban agribusiness, especially in the sugarcane fields and vineyards. More than 20,000 people were killed as prisoners of war."

The objective of Roca was to get land for his investors, the wealthy families that would buy parts of Patagonia on pre-sale and help fund the military campaigns. Over 40 years the cacique chief Calfucurá (*calfu* meaning 'blue', *curá* meaning 'stone') kept the Argentinean army limited to half of what is now Buenos Aires province, making peace treaties and fierce combats from the pampas all the way to the Andes. Exercising a masterful diplomacy with several Argentine governments, he arrived at the east side of the Andes in the mid-19th century and took leadership of the native tribes who were building a strong union there. He is the Mapuche chief with the most legends to his name. It's estimated that he lived around 100 years and that he had a blue stone that protected him and gave him powers such as the ability to ask favours of the spirits (including asking for rain and snow during the battles in order to make rivals run away), that he rode a horse of seven colours, and that he could be present in different parts of the expansive territory that he ruled in short spaces of time, or even that he and his horse were able to fly. He was like his father, a *Wentekura* (translating as a high, or celestial, stone), a *lonko* (*lonko* means head, and is also the name for the tribal chief) and a great *toki* (leader of the warriors).

He was defeated in 1872 and died the next year, making a final request to his people "Don't let the *huinca* [white people, or foreigners] take Carhué". More than 200 cacique chiefs attended Calfucurá's succession.

According to the journalist and writer Osvaldo Bayer: "After the destruction of the people of the south 41 million hectares were distributed to 1,843 landowners". This expansion of the territory lasted for another 50 years, with land being redistributed away from the Mapuche communities into the 21st century, especially after shale oil and gas reserves were discovered. With the announcement of a new reservoir of oil found by YPF in 2011 the conflicts grew again and many Mapuche families were victims of evictions after private companies claimed ownership of the lands. Vaca Muerta (a total area of 30,000 square kilometres) and Loma de La Lata (that occupies 36,000 hectares of land, and is the largest oil reserve in Argentina and one of the largest on the continent) are situated in territories that the Mapuche people claim as their ancestral lands. If the government complied with Convention 169 they should have consulted with the indigenous residents about the use of these lands.

A WAY OF BEING

"What was defending a people who had no major cities or buildings, even temples?" asks the professor of history and aesthetics, Gastón Soublette, who then answers: "The Incas couldn't conquer Mapuches, and later they fought for three centuries against European armies. They fought to defend their paradise, the land where they live. Their greatest creation is a special kind of humanity, a unique way of being. The words for man and woman have a beautiful story. Lituche, the first man, was made and thrown from the sky by the creator of everything, and he fell asleep on the land. The woman, Domo, was made shaped from a bright star, and she was put softly in the land by the creator. She is the one that awakes the man, and by her steps the flowers and the trees grew." Today the Mapuche people fight again to preserve what they consider sacred.

TRADITIONS

The communities still are, as in antiquity, matriarchal and under the authority of a *lonko* or cacique, who consults with the *machis* (healers) and the *werken* (spokesperson). Fabric is their most developed craft and is exclusively done by the females. The *ñerefé* (knitters) perform their work using two types of loom, which remain almost unchanged since prehistoric times: the vertical loom (*witral*) used to weave *matras* (blankets) and ponchos, and another known as the pampas loom, which allows them to make double-sided designs for *cincha* (horse tack) and *fajas* (belts).

An old game that continues today is *chueca*, which is played by men from when they're very young. It's a kind of hockey which teams play with sticks and a small ball, and where physical confrontation is allowed. If you let the ball go down the side of the court you must then defeat your opponent before getting the ball, and can pull their hair to throw them to the ground, a move known as *lonkeada*.

The Mapuche were not mining people and so would obtain silver by bartering with criollos or the Spanish, exhanging their cows and textiles for silver that they would then melt to make jewellery. The Mapuche are highly-skilled *retrafe* (silversmiths). They would then trade that jewellery back to the whites in exchange for more silver or goods. However, some of this jewellery would remain in the tribe. For instance, every woman receives a piece of jewellery when they are born and at specific moments in their life when they receive another made especially to tell their story. During the campaign led by Roca, most artisans were killed and their jewellery was stolen and sold to collectors, or even melted or lost (though some did end up in museums). This tradition was revived in the late 20th century by ICIA (Argentine Institute of Indigenous Culture) who worked with young people in workshops to re-teach these skills.

As for religion, ceremonies like *nguillatun*, *kamarikun* and *rogation*, where Nguechen (the god of the people) is thanked for the new crops and pleas are made for a better yield next year, are still held. These prayers that last between two and four days are celebrated by each family in their sacred land between the months of December and March.

In Mapuche everything has its own divine spirit, and music and instruments have a

Kultrun

big spiritual importance. In his book about the Mapuche the researcher Omar Lobos points out: "Nobody crosses a river, or takes fruit from a tree without asking prior permission to the river or the tree. That same feeling translates to the *tayillo* sacred chant. Not everyone can sing it, the chant exists inside of things and people, but it takes a lot of knowledge to take it out and express it properly. Every singer finds a way in any single moment to sing it".

The instruments are sacred and personal. For example,

the *kultrun*, a drum made with leather, has to be destroyed when its owner dies. The *trutruka* is a cane of between 4 and 8 meters length, covered with horse guts and with a cow's horn on the edge that amplifies the sound. *Kull kull* is also made with a cow's horn, but is a shorter wind instrument with a mouthpiece.

LILY FROM THE PAMPAS

Ceferino Namuncurá is set to become the first Mapuche saint. His case is similar to only one other in the world, Saint Catherine Tekakwitha, who was the 'Lily' among the mohawks. She is a patron saint of Montreal, and was an Algonquin/Mohawk laywoman, as well as the daughter of an indigenous chief who had been baptized by catholics.

Ceferino Namuncurá

Ceferino was the son of Manuel Namuncurá, whom after the chief Calfucurá died led the rest of the Salinas Grandes *lonkos*, who were the last southern chiefs without state to fight the government. In 1884 they would surrender, signing a peace treaty with Manuel being appointed a colonel in the Argentine army.

Ceferino was the next in line to be a *lonko*, continuing the family line of the Kurá dynasty, but instead chose to be a priest after going to a catholic school in Buenos Aires. Originally named Morales by his father, in honour of one of his friends, he was renamed by the priests as Ceferino, alluding to the Italian word *zaffirino* for sapphirine, a type of rock. After all, he was the littlest of the stone dynasty. He was spoiled by the priests, who called him 'Lily from the pampas', a clear repetition of a strategy that the priests knew from their Canadian colleagues. At just 17 years old he contracted tuberculosis and travelled to Italy as his teachers thought he would heal better in Turin, where he could also continue to study. He would meet Pope Pío XII, but unfortunately died in Rome after just a year away.

When his remains arrived in Argentina in 1924, people started paying tribute to Ceferino, offering their prayers, with many miracles being attributed to these intercessions. By the time the 60s had arrived a postage stamp with Ceferino's image on it had become hugely popular and people would go on pilgrimages to his grave asking and thanking for miracles.

For 83 years Ceferino was a 'popular saint', venerated by the people (mostly by the working class), but not recognized by the Vatican. However in November of 2007 the papal's envoy, Cardinal Tarcisio Bertone, beatified Ceferino Namuncurá before more than 100,000 people at a ceremony in Chimpay, Río Negro, his birthplace. This beatification, or blessing, is the certification of virtues by the pope and an official sign that they can be honoured with worship, as well as the essential step before that person is canonized as a saint.

The myth around Ceferino grows every day, but only time will tell what happens to his memory. His face is idolized by many people who ignore the past of his family.

STOLEN BONES

Inacayal was one of the last native chiefs to resist the military in Patagonia. He led an army of 3,000 men to the south, to a region known as the country of apples, where he fought alongside the great chief Sayhueque and surrendered in 1884. After being taken prisoner he was exhibited at the Natural Science Museum in La Plata, which is where he ultimately died. His body would later be dissected and he would be exhibited once more in separate glass cases in the Museum. In 2014 his mortal remains were returned to his community in Chubut. The historian Walter Delrio, CONICET researcher and professor at the National University of Río Negro, investigated the taking of aboriginal prisoners as slaves, for prostitution and their use by families and industries across the country, as well as the use of their mortal remains for scientific research without any scruples. "This restitution closes a very complex process, not only referring to the management of anthropological collections in museums, but on the construction of the Argentine state concerning indigenous peoples. Tens of thousands of adults and children were taken into pillboxes that functioned as concentration camps for further distribution to cities, tanneries, wine industries, mills, harvest, public works, as servants for families, and also enrolled in the army and navy," he stated.

The researcher defines this as "genocidal policies and practices, both by the government and civil society: the distribution of the [indigenous] was entrusted to ladies of charity, the Catholic church baptized them by changing names, and the godparents were in fact alleged adopters. After thousands of indigenous died [in the custody of their 'adopters'], family ties with survivors were dissolved and the state sought to disband the people. Not only did individuals physically disappear but they tried to wipe out entire villages, what we speak of as genocide".

MAPUCHES IN ARGENTINEAN CULTURE

José de San Martin crossed the Andes to fight for the liberty of Chile and Peru, wearing a poncho made by Mapuche women, from the family of the *toki* Wentekurá, the indigenous leader that helped the general get across the mountains. The Mapuches considered San Martin a native with many historians affirming that his mother was indigenous. 100 years later Carlos Gardel would perform his first successful European tour wearing a poncho, and with a haircut very much like the one Mapuches adopted in the city: short and with lots of gel to stop it from getting fuzzy. Gardel knew personally Ceferino, who was a few years ahead of him at the same school and had heard him sing in the school choir. Ceferino was a soprano who won two annual awards in school competitions; Gardel, on the other hand, was not mentioned in the school archives as an outstanding singer at all. In the golden age of tango, Gardel would become one of the three most acclaimed tango singers, along with Ignacio Corsini and Agustín Magaldi. Juan Epumer played guitar on record and toured with Magaldi, and was in fact the grandson of the *rankulche* chief Epumer. On many of his album credits, Epumer's name would be written as "Espumer" in an attempt to hide his native name.

Ernesto 'Che' Guevara's nickname popularised a native word that means person, as in *pehuen che* (people from pehuen), *huiliche che* (people from the south) and Mapuche (people from the earth). Soldiers took the word from indigenous territories to Buenos Aires and there it stuck, becoming even more widespread when adopted in the *lunfardo* slang that was becoming increasingly popular in tango. *Lunfardo* used words created in jails, that were combined with African and indigenous words such as 'che'. 'Gualicho' is another popular word that, to the Mapuches, means an 'evil spirit', a possessor of one's spirit, but is commonly used by many Argentines as a synonym for spell. Following a touristic boom in Patagonia in the 20th century many children who were not part of Mapuche families were baptized with Mapuche words like Nahuel (tiger), Nehuen (properly 'newen', meaning strength) or Ailén (luz).

The first musician to perform traditional songs from the Mapuche oral culture was Aimé Painé who toured across Europe and Latin America, but died in 1987 at the age of 44 during a tour of Paraguay. She was an important figure in the visibilization of the Mapuche nation. María Gabriela Epumer, who died in 2003, was a Mapuche descendant (the granddaughter of Juan Epumer) who played guitar in the band of Charly García during the 90s, and who died in 2003. Her older brother Lito also played guitar with a long history in rock and jazz rock fusions, such as being a part of Spinetta Jade. Artists like Luisa Calcumil and Beatriz Pichi Malén, who although they are not directly related to Mapuche people also helped spread Mapuche traditions through their records and live shows.

Today Juan Namuncurá, who was a *werken* (Mapuche spokesperson) for 18 years, has produced several publications, books, records, art exhibitions and other activities related to native traditions and heritage, in addition to working with communities to launch the first political party of indigenous people in Argentina, while continuing to work as a musician and record producer.

In his recent book *The Argentina of the Caciques. Or the Country that Never Happened*, which collects together letters written by indigenous chiefs to the Argentinean state, the anthropologist Carlos Martinez Sarasola writes: "The native chiefs saw it possible to build and share a country with the *huincas* [foreigners], but Argentina didn't want to [share], and tried to eliminate the natives as hard as they could". Now that the country has celebrated 200 years it seems that Argentina has still not learned to live with its native people.

CO-EXISTENCE IS SACRED

THE RESISTANT RHYTHMS OF JUAN NAMUNCURÁ

by Pablo Andrés Bobadilla

translated by Danny Concha

Juan Namuncurá is a Mapuche/Aymara musician, producer and political activist. In both music and politics he is gambling on finding a new level of harmony.

"There is one value in life: that co-existence is sacred. It is sacred to everything, whether man, rock or animal you have to care for it, foster it and nurture it, never harm or break it. Co-existence is all about a shared appreciation. There are families that still give thanks each day to the animals that sustain them, while others have lost their conscience. Our decadence is thanks to this contamination of mankind," says Juan Arévalo Sgró Namuncurá as he prepares the *mate* in the living room of his house in Buenos Aires, keeping a close eye to see that his youngest son finishes his homework before he plays video-games, meanwhile his eldest son practices cello and his wife

alternates between reading a book and cooking dinner.

Juan is a descendent of one of the earliest-documented dynasties in local indigenous history. His forefather, Manuel Namuncurá, was the last great Mapuche *toki* to stand up to the state of Argentine and following his defeat, the pampas and Patagonia became unified territories with new borders imposed on their family history. "My parents met in the city of La Plata where they were studying. My father was an Aymara dentist, born in Bolivia, and my mother a Mapuche born in Argentina who studied law but later became a teacher. My birthplace was determined by my Aymara side, and my Mapuche family took care of my upbringing. I lived in Cochabamba until I was three and then moved permanently to Argentina. I don't believe that the concept of a nation can ever capture those small differences that exist between native communities".

Juan is now attempting to bring together the two roles which he has been keeping apart for the past 15 years; that of the artist and the political activist. He explains that "Argentina is far behind in terms of human rights, often covering up such blatant crimes against humanities as the genocide inflicted on native settlements. There seems to be an obsession with trying to paint us as a minority when in reality, it's the native people who form the majority."

"Life is strictly artistic and time is art. I found the balance within the circle of life when I realised that I could be both a political and artistic figure. We formed the collective 'Pueblos de la Madre Tierra' and now I'm looking for new ways to access democracy in a way that complies with Convention 169 [of the International Labour Organization] concerning the integration, respect and consultation with native communities."

Tell us about your upbringing. Were your native traditions passed down to you from childhood?

As the child of educated natives, I could see right away how uncomfortable the European immigrants who governed our town were when it came to interacting with an indigenous dentist who spoke five languages or an Indian school head mistress. They simply didn't fulfil that stereotype of the 'natives.'

I was taught the customs of my ancestors, but it was never imposed on me. In our culture the family passes down traditions but in the end it's all about making that connection with the earth. We would make ceremonies to mother nature, we would work the land and we would keep up-to-date with all developments.

When did you discover your calling as an artist?

When I was five, I took piano classes in Río Negro with a neighbour who played in my uncle's band. Whenever I heard them play, the piano would always captivate me and so, my parents sent me off to learn. Not long afterwards though, my teacher got married and stopped giving classes so I began studying under her piano master, an

Italian gentleman who used to be the organist at the Cathedral in Prague before he fled Europe during the horrors of the war. He'd ended up in Villa Regina, a small town full of Italian expats. That's how I came to receive the biggest dose of Western music in my life. My neighbours remember him as this strict and forceful man, but to me he was the opposite! I had a wonderful time with him and he taught me with great affection.... it's like he was one person to me, and another to the rest... I'll never really understand.

Who were your musical influences?

Through my teacher I began discovering all the classics as well as less mainstream composers. I started listening to the romantics like Chopin, Liszt and Tchaikovsky and when I heard the triple vinyl of *Close to the Edge* by Yes in 1973, which begins with extracts from Stravinsky's "The Firebird" and goes into a chorus whose sound was completely alien to me (years later I'd learn that it was a melltron), that's when I started listening to impressionists like Bartók. After that I got really into serialism until I came across the minimalism of Philip Glass. I needed to find a sound that could represent my own ideas, environments and climate. How do I transmit a lake, or a mountain or the wind? That's when I started experimenting with synthesisers and MIDI.

In 1979, I went to Córdoba to study engineering and fine art. Towards the end of the 70s and throughout the 80s there was a debate about the extent to which an institution could contain a talent. I started reading and asking questions about art, mathematics and engineering all at the same time. What even is the note 'do' and why do we all play under this sonic code? This code corresponds to a logarithm and a quadratic equation, the twelfth root of two, which happens because we are developing a twelve-note harmony. Having this knowledge for one thousand years has stopped us approaching new ways to make harmonies. Why can't we think outside the box? Life is about more than just formalities. I didn't finish any of my courses, but I never stopped investigating.

When Aimé Painé first appeared, how did you react to her work?

I first came across Aimé in the 1970s at the Choele Choel Festival; she was keen to meet my mother. Then, some years later I went over to visit my mother and the next night an old lady, who we found drinking *mate* with another woman. That woman was Aimé Painé and we got talking and I was telling her about my experiments with synthesisers. "We need more people like you for continuity's sake" she told me, and that encouraged me to keep composing. Her first record really lifted my spirits. I found the content beautiful but the sound quality was really bad as it had been done without any support and with a purely anthropological vision; it needed a record producer. That's when I got the [initial] idea of doing something with Aimé Painé's music myself. Then many years later I was given an audio recording from Mar de Plata which I digitised and edited as part of a series of records that I was producing under the title *De Lo Profundo de la Madre Tierra* (From The Depths of Mother Earth). It featured previously unreleased tracks of hers, and the most beautiful thing is that they are explanations of the truth that she would tell us through her singing. It's a live recording which presents life to people just as she used to: she was a great storyteller.

MIXER

In Buenos Aires in the 1990s Juan got involved in the creation of the Latin American Grammy's and pushed for the creation of a native Grammy, but saw how the industry produced and promoted folk records that didn't have much to do with native music and culture. He had his first child and separated from his wife, and then married his current wife and companion, the artist and researcher Susana Frank with whom he founded ICIA and completed several projects on native culture. Juan won repeated prizes as a composer for cinema and theatre, and even composed a symphonic score which was performed at the Atlanta 1996 Olympic Games, but he never won the support needed to bring out his own record and so, dedicated himself instead to mixing and producing the records of other musicians. He mixed two notable hardcore punk records, The *Art of Romance* by Fun People (recorded by Steve Albini), and *Single Club* by Loquero, and he worked with pop artists such as Julieta Venegas and Alejandro Lerner, always keeping his eyes and ears open. This millennium, Juan has worked in international forums like the UN, developed workshops for the native youth population in various regions of Argentina, had a second child who has taken his mother's German citizenship and recorded his his debut album, *Energía Solar* (Solar Energy). That album was released by his own label Piedra Azul Records (Blue Stone, like Calfucura), with his eldest son contributing, playing several instruments on the album such as the Hindu *tabla*. His music combines avant garde electronic influences with Mapuche language songs and acoustic instruments from different cultures. If you understand the concept of Daft Punk, you could think of Namuncurá's music as 'Daftpuche' to arrive at a possible definition of his work.

Which native artists have inspired you?

Native music has always been a part of me: before, I lived it through my community, through our ceremonies and celebrations, and now I have access to it through the internet which has shown me the work of native artists and enthusiasts alike. Just like me, those Russian classical composers that I so admire would seek to use their tools (in their case, the orchestra) to forge sounds that evoke the rural folk music of their environment. I'll always carry the artistic attitude of John Trudel close to my heart, whose appearance in films gave exposure to his poetic output, his records... he was a real discovery for me.

I respect the work of the label Real World, and other groups such as Deep Forest or Enya who managed to reach a wide range of audiences with music that respected tradition whist being modern at the same time, and initiatives like Live Aid, who clearly recognise the social value of art; it prioritises world health over fame and fortune. I'd spent the past 15 years trying to separate my music from my activism and eventually I decided that I can and should do both things at once. It's time for all people of mother earth to unite, to share and spread our cultures and to work towards co-existence.

CONTRIBUTORS

Adam Fry is an environmental educator who has lived and worked in various Latin American countries. Currently based in Nottingham after two years in Montevideo, he is especially interested in youth culture, environmental affairs and the Southern Cone.

Alan Chac is an Argentinean photographer working in both analogue and digital formats. His work focuses on structures, lines and perspectives, with architecture forming his main point of inspiration. He is currently based in La Plata.

Alan Courtis is a musician and composer also working in the field of 'disabilities'. He has a degree in Science of Communication and writes articles for books and culture magazines. He is currently based in Buenos Aires.

Alexandra Nataf is a French writer and translator currently studying at UCL. Speaking French, English and Spanish, a musician herself, she loves music, movies, travelling and discovering new cultures.

Amaya García-Velasco is an independent researcher and music journalist based in Puerto Rico. She holds an MA in Popular Music and Culture from the University of Western Ontario in London, Canada.

Ana Young is a BA Spanish and Italian student at UCL in London who embraces Latin American culture, using her passion for it to reconnect with her Brazilian heritage. She is involved with many events and projects hoping to propagate Latin American culture in the UK.

Bennett Tucker is an independent writer and researcher focusing on 20th century European and Latin American modernism. Based in the US, he's an avid traveler as well as book and furniture collector.

Claire Green is a PhD Law student at Queen Mary University, where she is researching the use of music by political prisoners in Northern Ireland. She holds an MA in Spanish from the University of Glasgow.

Danny Concha is a London-based Modern Languages (BA) student at the University of Oxford and University College London. He is passionate about Latin American literature and film and holds positions as editor and translator for various cultural magazines.

Denise Luciana de Fátima Braz is a Portuguese Language and Literature teacher at the Pontifical Catholic University of Minas Gerais in Belo Horizonte, Brazil. She is currently pursuing her masters in Social Anthropology from the Department of Philosophy and Literature at the University of Buenos Aires.

Diane Ghogomu is a North American artist and educator who has lived in Buenos Aires for six years. She received her degree in African American studies at Harvard University. In 2014 she codirected, filmed and produced a documentary called *Buenos Aires Rap*. She is currently working on her second film about the experience of Afro-descendents in Buenos Aires.

Ellen Gordon is a freelance journalist and translator, with a special interest in Latin American culture and art. She has completed a BA in Hispanic Studies from King's College London and is currently based in Colombia.

Emma Canlin is an enthusiastic designer, with a particular interest in illustration, branding, narrative and crafts. She is currently studying at Nottingham Trent University and specializes in graphic design and illustration.

George Kafka is a writer, editor and researcher with a special interest in Latin American architecture and urbanism. His work has been featured in Metropolis, uncube, The Spaces and Huck and he is currently working towards an MSc in Urban Studies at UCL.

Jacob Lassar is an Austrian-born, Brazilian based-journalist, digital marketing consultant and hiking guide, currently exploring the musical and natural landscape of Latin America.

Jessica Sequeira is a writer and translator living in Buenos Aires.

Juan Data is a music journalist and DJ born and raised in Buenos Aires, Argentina, who's been residing in Northern California for the past 15 years. When he's not obsessively sorting his large vinyl collection, he reads comic books, rides bicycles and skateboards and practices archery.

Lee Hodges is an illustrator, who likes his work to dance off the page. Music, folklore and Latin culture are major sources of inspiration. View his work at leeho.co.uk

Lina Samoili is a writer and researcher, currently based in London. She has worked in various film festivals, such as Argentine Film Festival and Sheffield Doc/Fest and she holds an MA in Film and Television Studies from the University of Bristol.

Lorna Scott Fox is a translator from French and Spanish, journalist, critic and editor, currently based in London after living in Mexico and Spain for twenty years.

Matias Recharte is a musician and educator from Peru based in Toronto, Ontario. He holds an MA in Ethnomusicology from York University and is currently studying a PhD in Music Education at the University of Toronto.

Miguel David Grinberg was born in Buenos Aires in 1937. He is a journalist, poet and writer who has published over 50 books and is currently preparing his first poetry record. He was the first journalist to promote the Argentine rock movement, created the first ecology magazine in the country and still hosts a radio show and meditation groups.

Milena Annecchiarico is a Doctor of Anthropology at the University of Buenos Aires, where she is also an investigator for the Institute of Anthropological Sciences, as well as being an independent film-maker. Since 2009 she has developed research projects relating to the African presence in Latin America and the Caribbean.

Nicholas Nicou is a professional freelance French and Spanish to English translator. He is the London Sub-Editor of Sounds and Colours.

Nick MacWilliam is a writer and editor based between London, Santiago and Buenos Aires. He regularly contributes to Sounds and Colours, where he is the Assistant Editor, as well as several other publications. He is also co-editor of Alborada Magazine, the UK's first print magazine devoted entirely to Latin America.

Pablo Andrés Bobadilla conspires for universal harmony. He was born in Comodoro Rivadavia in Patagonia in 1984, bit now lives and works in Buenos Aires City. He is a journalist, music editor and producer but is becoming more and more dedicated to organic farming and DIY carpentry.

Prisca Gayles is a doctoral student at the Lozano-Long Institute of Latin American Studies at the University of Texas. She has a degree in Hispanic Languages and Literature from the University of Pittsburgh and a Master's in Latin American Studies from the University of South Florida.

Sandwich Gogogoch are Alejandro Leonelli and Malen Di Santo, two creative Argentine designers who set up a micro studio and workshop. Back in 2010 they designed the original Sounds and Colours logo. It's great to be working with them again.

Russell Slater is the founder/editor of Sounds and Colours.

Stephanie Kennedy lived and worked in Latin America for seven years as a journalist, covering issues such as indigenous land rights, social struggles, government and foreign policy. She is now based in London and works for Spanish and Latin American cultural centre and school, Battersea Spanish.

Vivian Mota has been working in illustration for the past 10 years after studying graphic design and fashion. She lives in São Paulo.

CONTEMPORARY ARGENTINE MUSIC MIXTAPE

BY DOMA TORNADOS

As a special treat for everyone who has bought this book we are extremely happy to offer this free-to-download mixtape created by Argentine producer Doma Tornados, a hugely influential tropical bass project based in Spain. The mix features new music from Mi Amigo Invencible, Puelche, Lauphan, Sobrenadar, Chancha Vía Circuito, The Peronists, El Hijo de la Cumbia, Marcelo Fabian and many other emerging and established names from the Argentine music scene.

Download from http://bit.ly/2epdkJX

QUE CANCHERO

NEW SOUNDS OF ARGENTINA

1. Lauphan – Movimiento
Lauphan thrives on the *música litoraleña* of Argentina, taking it to a cosmic dimension. The chants of villagers, campfires, rural workers and the soundscapes of the interior all appear frequently in his songs.

2. Faauna – La Ruleta (Previously Unreleased)
Faauna is a pioneering digital cumbia group from Argentina. Two MCs with a love for electronic music, they pump out beats from the world's *barrios*, with lyrics that oscillate between the metaphysical and the shamanistic.

3. Lulacruza – Uno Resuena
This Argentine/Colombian duo have been performing together for over 10 years but it's on their last few albums that their soulful, healing take on folktronica has really knitted together, making music full of feeling and with a deep connection to the natural world.

4. Mariana Päraway – Marinera
Hailing from Mendoza, Päraway's music navigates between pop, folk, electronica and experimentation, creating a mix that is both local and universal. Strings, wind instruments, guitars and electronic flourishes circle her crystalline voice for a dense and vibrant sound.

5. Julio y Agosto – Era Tarde
Since appearing on the scene Julio y Agosta have surprised with their particular approach to music and their septet formation. Vocals, Spanish and electric guitars, violins, trombone, upright bass, percussion and keyboards create an eclectic yet familiar sound.

6. Soema Montenegro – Gota de Rocío
One of the great contemporary folk voices of Argentina, maintaining traditions of yore while also writing beautiful melodies and lyrics. This is taken from 2016's *Ave del Cielo*.

7. Santiago Córdoba – Mamila
Alongside his work in nuevo tango group Violentago, Córdoba has maintained a solo career rich with textures and ideas, evidenced by his latest album *Corso*, from which this is taken.

8. Femina – Buen Viaje
Channeling hip-hop into *nueva canción* for a style that resembles the borderless sound of Manu Chao and directness of Ana Tijoux, Femina are a new group with a bright future.

9. Arbolceniza – Arbolceniza
This Argentine duo who grew up in Spain mix the sound of the ballad and Latin American folklore with pop music. The result has given birth to a sensorial trip that is both transcendent and connected to its origins.

10. Shaman Y Los Pilares de La Creación – Sed
Shaman y los Pilares de la Creación have created a ritual music with clear ethnic origins. Their sound fuses elements of folkloric Patagonian music with rock. It's a stripped, minimalistic brew, rich in textures and rhythm with a voice hollering as if from the middle of the mountain range.

11. Sara Hebe & Ramiro Jota – No Puedo
Sara Hebe began writing her own songs by crafting lyrics and melodies over rhythms she found on the internet. Together with Ramiro Jota, she is using rap as a platform to explore styles such as reggae, cumbia, dancehall and electronica.

12. Mi Amigo Invencible – La Danza de Los Principiantes
Originally from Mendoza, Mi Amigo Invencible have become one of the key names in Argentina's indie rock scene. They create sinewy post-punk, offering an original reinterpretation of folklore from the region.

13. Nación Ekeko – Guarania
With *La Danza*, Nación Ekeko elevated himself to the top table of electronic music producers exploring Andean melodies and post-digital cumbia beats. Using traditional Latin American instruments, "Guarania"is one of the most club-ready tracks on the album.

14. Los Espíritus – La Crecida
Los Espíritus are the sound of a wild night: urban tales, neon lights and smoke billowing over from the factories. With a base of incessant grooves and dense atmosphere they create their own Rio de la Plata take on psychedelia.

15. Juan Namuncurá – Quedate
A true original, there are few artists who sound quite like Namuncurá. On his sole (hard-to-find) album *Solar Energía*, he unites the unlikely influences of electronica and rave-influenced techno with natural symbolism and hispanic and indigenous languages.

16. Alan Courtis – Cuero del Alba (Previously Unreleased)
With the iconic group Reynols, Courtis pushed the limits of performance, experimental rock and the expectations that come with being in a band. "Cuero del Alba" is an alternative take from *B-Rain Folklore*, a recent album that plays with the idea of Argentine folklore.

***

Produced by Concepto Cero and Sounds and Colours

Compiled by Ángel Clemente Del Re, Nicolas Madoery and Russell Slater

Mastered by Jõao Carvalho

Design by Sandwich Gogogoch

ALSO AVAILABLE
Cultural Guides to South America

SOUNDS AND COLOURS PERU

Book, CD and DVD taking a look at contemporary Peruvian culture, and the country's musical, cultural and folkloric icons. From the indigenous traditions of the Andes, to the country's reinstatement of its Afro-Peruvian identity, and on to the contemporary art, film and music that thrives on the coast, we show another side of Peru.

Includes DVD of Peruvian folkloric culture films by acclaimed film-maker Vincent Moon

SOUNDS AND COLOURS BRAZIL

Book and CD focused on Brazilian music and culture, covering topics as diverse as the new music scene in Rio de Janeiro, Gilvan Samico's rural art, the Brazilian film industry, carnival in Recife, contemporary art and much more. It is the only book on the market that thoroughly explores contemporary culture in Brazil.

"You need to get it"--Cerys Matthews, BBC Radio 6 Music

MÁS...

• Various Artists: Sonidos Raíces del Peru (Music)
• Nillo & Sentidor + Friends – SIBÖ Revisited (Music)
• Sounds and Colours Colombia (Book and CD; To Be Reissued in 2017/18)